AN UNCOMPROMISED LIFE

Colleen Gallagher

AN UNCOMPROMISED
life

Overcome Trauma & Heartbreak, Experience the
Unexplainable, and Truly Fall in Love with Life

NEW YORK

LONDON • NASHVILLE • MELBOURNE • VANCOUVER

An Uncompromised Life

Overcome Trauma and Heartbreak, Experience the Unexplainable, and Truly Fall in Love with Life

Published in New York, New York, by Morgan James Publishing. Morgan James is a trademark of Morgan James, LLC. www.MorganJamesPublishing.com

ISBN 9781631952760 paperback
ISBN 9781631952777 eBook
Library of Congress Control Number: 2020942354

Cover Design by:
Megan Dillon
megan@creativeninjadesigns.com

Interior Design by:
Christopher Kirk
www.GFSstudio.com

Morgan James is a proud partner of Habitat for Humanity Peninsula and Greater Williamsburg. Partners in building since 2006.

Get involved today! Visit
MorganJamesPublishing.com/giving-back

To the universe and to myself.
And to Ella.

Table of Contents

Acknowledgments

T hank you to Anna Allen (Anna Naturalista), Ivonne Dela-
flor, Pam Shorter, Veronica Villanueva, Audrie Dawn,
Charles Gallagher, Sam Spidell, Ben Beard, Dr. Kristie
Holmes, Nicole Scheier, Larry Spagnola, Erin Badour and the
Soul of Ella's dad. To all my other friends, mentors, family
members and magical people who appeared along this journey
whom guided me through this—you know who you are.

I'd also like to extend a thank you to Morgan James Publishing and Cortney Donelson for publishing and editing *An
Uncompromised Life*.

I am eternally grateful.

Introduction

am beyond grateful for every person who guided me through this experience and for the whole experience itself.

To my sweetest Ella,

I'm so sorry that you couldn't make it to live this beautiful life as an earth angel, as my beautiful daughter.

During the six beautiful days you were in my stomach, I could feel you bouncing around. I could feel your contagious energy that would have captivated so many people.

I looked at my life twenty years ahead, a life with the parents you would have had. I would have robbed you of experiencing a life with two parents who are in love. I would have robbed you of my unconditional love.

You would have seen your mother suffering, living a life that wasn't meant for her because of you. I would have sacrificed my well-being for you and repeated the same generational pattern that has played out time and time again.

Ella, I love you more than you'll ever know.

Yet, in making my decision, I chose you and gave you a far greater gift than being present to fulfill a life that would have caused you suffering.

XOXO

To every woman out there,

Remember, it's your duty to choose yourself first—always. Because if you don't choose you, the generation behind you is learning that pattern, a message that says they must sacrifice their souls to hopefully one day obtain peace.

Because as women, it's our right to choose ourselves. I don't see this as an option.

Please enjoy every moment of this beautiful book, empowering yourself to live *An Uncompromised Life* so you change your life, inspire those around you, and remember how to experience the unexplainable.

Author's Note

I n this book, you will encounter a story that will activate you, educate you, connect with you, move you, inspire you, and most importantly, empower you to remember just how incredible your life can be.

In the first chapter, I share an in-depth story about what happens when you live a life that compromises who you truly are to please someone else. The other twelve chapters dive into the twelve lessons that were revealed to me throughout my life—lessons about what it takes to truly live *An Uncompromised Life*.

Through this story, I hope to guide you to live into your soul's calling, live out your ultimate potential, understand what it takes to live an extraordinary life, and truly experience love in a way you never knew possible. Those end goals are exactly what I learned through these life lessons, which I share here.

CHAPTER 1

An Unplanned Miracle

Part 1

My mum and I went for a walk the Tuesday before Thanksgiving. I love the ocean and the beach—something about the sand squishing between my toes and the sound of the beautiful ocean going in and out. The way the sun rays hit your face. For me, it's magical.

We were in Florida, getting together for the holiday, and my mum and I went for the walk and then sat on the beach. We sat there for about two hours. I was processing a lot of anxiety, fear, and uneasiness about this guy I was seeing.

I couldn't get him or the relationship out of my head. I was obsessing over this guy, and I couldn't seem to move through it. I was so unhappy with the situation. I couldn't tell if the guy liked me or didn't like me, and I knew I was compromising parts of myself to meet this guy's needs. So I felt depleted and unsure of myself.

Yet, it was something I had created all in my head because I was so disconnected from my heart—from recognizing I was never going to be at ease with the situation.

Suddenly, my mum asks, "Colleen, can I change the subject?"

"Yes."

Part of me felt happy to change the topic, and part of me couldn't stop the thoughts racing through my head about this guy. When she started to speak, I felt like I had just come up for a breath of fresh air after trying to hold my breath under water for five minutes.

Finally, she said, "You know, I have figured out the reason I got pregnant with a girl."

Curiously, I asked, "Why?"

She responded, "Otherwise, I would have been stuck with all men." My dad's family has five brothers and one sister, and none of his siblings are married except for my dad, and my mum was an only child too, like me. She has no living family left. If she hadn't had a daughter—me—she would have had only men in her life.

In that moment, my heart sank, and I felt like I wanted to go right back under the water, wishing I hadn't come up for that breath of fresh air. This conversation with my mum brought a lot of clarity to concepts I'd been studying the past two years. One of them was something called generational lineage, and in that moment, I understood the meaning of it. I realized that my life, my mum's life, and many other women within their own lineage were not living their lives for themselves.

The comment my mum made empowered me to do a deep dive research analysis into understanding myself and my DNA on a whole new level. When we truly understand ourselves, we have the opportunity to change our lives drastically. I am so excited to share with you why this comment my mum made was so impactful and monumental in my growth and healing within four months of letting my child go. However, before I get to that . . . as you read through this book, there are some terms you should know so that you can receive the full impact this story can offer for your life.

Generational Lineage

From my understanding, generational lineage impacts us from seven generations up, and we impact seven generations down. Emotional trauma, wounding, financial problems, love relationships, family wealth and debt, along with other things are all passed down to our souls from our family lineage before we incarnate in the physical world. We have two options: We either become aware of the subconscious DNA coding from our generational lineage and transmute the denser lineage passed to us, which allows us to create new opportunities for greater growth to be passed down to those still yet to come, or we avoid the generational lineage DNA passed down to us, live our life suffering from it, and pass it down to the lineage that is yet to come.

When my mum told me the reason she had a girl, I realized she gave birth to me so I could function as her survival guide in her life. I was her purpose for existing. However, this creates a subconscious codependent coding, where the child can feel that the mother needs the child more than the child can rely and depend on the mother. See my mum (and many other moms out there) are sourcing their love and happiness from their children instead of from within themselves.

When this happens, the child cannot come to the parent in need, in hope, or in tears. When mothers source self-purpose from children, a subconscious yet high expectation is placed on the children, expectations of perfection, happiness, and completeness. Again, this is not the mom's fault because they learned this from previous generational patterns and habits. Historically, generational lineage of women focused on women staying at home to care for the husband and children before caring for themselves.

Because of this generational lineage, I was raised with codependent looping, causing me to seek out partners—men—to fill that void of love and happiness. I was taught to do this by watching my mum source love and happiness from me. Not all women or men do this through relationships; some people turn to alcohol to fill the void, some to drugs, others to sports, still others to coffee, and some become workaholics. These are the offset problems, the symptoms, that occur when others model this codependent behavior for us.

Karmic Debt

There are numerous definitions for karmic debt. From my own experience, I believe its karma that others carry within themselves for reasons unknown to us, yet when we choose to closely intertwine with these individuals, we offer ourselves as mediums for their karma to flow through our life. This allows the person carrying the karma to receive the messages and growth opportunities they are meant to learn. It's called karmic debt because in past lifetimes (or even this current lifetime) we each have done wrong and right to others and that creates a debt of karma that will come back to us. Sometimes our karma (or other people's karma) can be so big or the lesson that is needed to be learned is so large that karmic debt comes through other people for them to learn the lessons.

For example, often in movies (and in real life), if people want revenge, they don't go after you, they go after the people you love. In doing so, they get you to do what they want. Well, the universe works like that sometimes.

Why?

We have been trained to care more about others than ourselves. So, the universe will have lessons come through the people who are closest to us, to teach us a lesson. When we are closely intertwined with someone who has a lot of karmic debt or a lot of lessons their soul needs to learn, we end up being part of the lesson someone else needs to experience for their karmic debt to be complete. Simultaneously, this happens with us, people can be close with us and they experience our karmic debt that we needed to learn. Everything is always a two-way street.

In this story I became that person who experienced the karmic debt of my mum and the child's dad, and they probably experienced some of my karmic debt while going through this experience. I firmly believe this unplanned pregnancy was to fulfill karmic debt and complete a soul contract, because there were lessons in this for everyone—including the Western medical field. However, I don't want to focus on everyone else's lessons; the point of *An Uncompromised Life* is we start to focus on us, because we are the most important person in our life. A huge part of my lesson in this was learning how to transmute the darkness I co-created in this event and shed light on it. From this place of shedding light on the darkness, we allow ourselves to co-create with other people. I believe this is how we heal and complete a karmic debt. In doing so, we get to evolve into a higher state of consciousness—if we choose, of course.

Co-Creation

There are many ways to explain co-creation, yet how I experience it myself is by this simple concept: Understand that nothing happens to you, everything is co-created by you with the universe for your highest growth. Everything that is existing around you—your relationships, your problems, your success, and everything else is something that you co-created with the universe. For example, if you are in debt, you co-created that—it did not just happen to you. If you are in an abusive relationship, you co-created that—it did not just randomly happen to you. If you have had success, you co-created that. Every thought, every word, every feeling you have is putting a vibration out into the universe, which is coming back to you in a certain frequency, birthing a co-creative relationship between you and the universe.

Everything that is happening around you is because of conscious or unconscious thoughts you are having about yourself, others, and life. For example, every perceived negative situation that has occurred to you is because you had negative thoughts and feelings at a conscious or subconscious level over a period of time that manifested the perceived negative event. The same goes for every positive experience—you allowed yourself to start thinking and feeling good about life, so life started to co-create with you and deliver good things to you. Everything always has a duality, there is never just a bad or just a good; both good and bad are always available, yet it is up to you to decide how you choose to receive the world.

The moment you start to become responsible to empower yourself to think thoughts that guide you to feel good and trust in the universe, then you start co-creating *An Uncompromised Life*.

Soul Contracts

Soul contracts have various meanings depending on who you talk to, yet the way I experience it and see my clients experience it is this: We have chosen to go through certain circumstances before incarnating here on the planet, and everything that happens "to" us is because we are completing a soul contract. Everything in our life—our relationships, health, careers—is because we created a soul contract that we agreed to go through in the human experience for our soul's evolution. This includes having cancer, going through a divorce, choosing the parents we have, money problems, career successes, etc. Nothing—I mean *nothing*—you go through or that happens to you is by accident; it is always because you are completing a contract you made with your soul to learn a lesson and evolve.

These contracts are so important to understand because they bind us to the collective whole of humanity. As I talked about in my first book, *Live Your Truth*, our basis for being alive is to feel connection with others. Connection can only occur when we share the hard times we have been through with others, because it guides us to understand that we have each gone through the same pain (which is the basis for our connection).

Yet, an even deeper meaning of how these soul contracts bind us to the greater collective humanity is this: Some of us may feel moved by animal cruelty, while others may feel passionate about eradicating human trafficking. Some may feel moved by poverty, while others may be passionate about sustainability efforts. The reason people are more moved by a specific topic over another is because they took on a soul contract where something in their soul's life (either past lifetimes or this one) has connected them to a social cause or social injustice. They went through some trauma that connects them to that specific greater cause.

The power of understanding your soul contracts is to understand that everything you have gone through is something you chose to go through. It is your job to focus on learning the lessons of why something occurred in your life, which leads to healing yourself. Then you can start providing solutions for the greater collective humanity problem that you and many other people are going through or have gone through.

We only complete soul contracts when we have fully learned the lesson a person or experience is meant to teach us, otherwise the same lesson will keep coming back through different experiences or people. For example, if you keep going in debt, you haven't learned your soul's contract with creating wealth, money, and abundance. However, once you have learned the lesson and completed the soul contract (or even karmic contract) you must cut the cord for the energetic ties that an experience or person has brought you. This way you are not carrying the heavy toxic emotional baggage that goes with the lesson; you are only carrying the gift the lesson has brought you.

Cord Cutting

What is a cord and how do we cut it?

Think of the umbilical cord that goes from your mother into what eventually becomes your belly button. Similarly, we each have connections (called energetic cords) that go from us to hundreds, thousands, perhaps even billions of people or things around the world. These cords can be subconscious or conscious. For every living thing or person we are closely intertwined with in the physical plane, we were somehow connected before the present moment—whether it be from another reality, previous lifetime, or simple scientific matter that composes human DNA.

The question becomes: How do we become aware of these energetic cords we have with people and things? And how do we remove the cords from things and people we do not want to be connected to?

Well, first you must understand there is a field of infinite possibilities available to you. Yet if you are energetically connected to your family and all the beliefs that they carry about being successful, you are going to be held back from reaching success.

If you are energetically attached to working a nine-to-five job, making $120K a year, and then one day retiring, you are going to miss seeing opportunities that could provide a greater life for you.

If you are in a relationship and that person's beliefs become your beliefs (perhaps they believe that starting a business is hard, and it takes a long time to make money), this can actually stop you from believing your dreams are possible. A workplace example may be cutting the cord of jealously if you are very jealous of someone for being a better employee.

The point of cutting the cord is so the toxic parts of you that are being brought out by someone or something, are being requested to leave from your conscious and subconscious mind. So moving forward you only hold the positive parts of the lessons someone or something was meant to bring to you. You can cut the cord with someone or something that is still in your life; you just would be cutting the cord of the toxic parts of you and the other person (or thing) that are not working toward your highest growth.

The key in cord cutting is becoming aware that the people and things you are closely intertwined with have an energetic impact on you—you are connected with their habits, beliefs, and thoughts as they are with yours, until you cut the cord.

So how do you cut the cord?

There are many ways to cut cords. In fact, you can go on YouTube and find tons of videos. The way I do it is: I close my eyes, imagine the person or thing that is causing me emotional instability, and I imagine the cord from his or her heart to my heart and my belly button. I then have the cord represent whatever it is I want to leave behind: codependency, jealously, anger, resentment, etc. I imagine a fire, consuming and dissolving the cords. Then, in my imagery, I slice the person's and my head off so that both of the toxic parts of us (which were existing in my world) pass away, and only the light can move forward within me.

I suggest imagining the cords being dissolved, rather than being cut because when you cut something, it can be sewn or put back together. When something dissolves, it's over; there is no coming back.

***

The morning after that walk on the beach in Florida, I woke up just crying and crying and crying. I do not think I have ever cried so hard before. It was at that moment, I knew I was pregnant. I truly believe one of the reasons my pregnancy happened like this, within less than twenty-four hours of what my mum shared on the beach, is because that activated the generational lineage coding for me to either pass it down to the next generation or stop it once and for all.

However, in this moment of intuitively knowing I was pregnant, I felt such a darkness come over me, a darkness I had never felt before in my whole life. I felt like I was in a pool of water that had just turned black. Because I was pregnant with this man's child—a guy who had other relationships with women. He was living with one woman, and I knew if I had this child, I was going to pass along the same generational pattern my mum had just made me aware of. In this same moment, I saw the whole karmic relationship tie that I was having with the child's dad, throughout the centuries . . . many lifetimes. It was in that moment, as tears were falling out of my eyeballs like the ocean running out of my eyes, that I closed my eyes and started to dissolve the deep, interwoven cord that had forever connected us together.

I realized if I had this baby, I would only be doing so in the hopes of feeling like there was a silver lining in this terrible situation of life in which I was existing. This was not the reality I wanted to live in, nor the reality I wanted to have a child in. I was crying because deep down, I knew this was a huge wakeup call. I needed to start loving myself and creating a real relationship with my soul in an effort to become the person I (am) meant to be.

Some of you may be asking, "Why weren't you more responsible so you didn't get pregnant in the first place?" And I have an answer.

At age fourteen, I had thyroid cancer, and it was communicated to me that I would need to increase my medication to ever get pregnant. Because of this, I never thought I needed to use measures to stop pregnancy from happening. I never had an issue in serious relationships I had been in before. I never knew the power of someone's intention to have a child could override medical doctors' suggestions. Because deep down, this man really wanted children. And deep down, at a subconscious level, I wanted to know I could have children. So naturally, this experience co-created itself in my life. His desire and my subconscious desire (with the added bonus of me compromising my soul to please this man) resulted in an unplanned pregnancy.

I was crying because I should have known this could be a possibility. Afterall, I too had used the power of my own intention to go off the medication the doctors told me I would be on for the rest of my life the previous three years. This all proves the power of your mind. Your mind can overcome any medical diagnosis from the Western medical field, as it has occurred twice in my life, and I've seen it occur countless times in other people's lives. However, in this moment of anger with the medical field, the emotion of internal gratitude was also birthed. I never knew it would be possible to become a mom, so I always shoved the idea out of my mind. Yet, through this the world showed me that I absolutely can become a mom—

when the time and the partner is right. From that simple shift in perspective I allowed myself to be guided to turn my anger into gratitude.

However, in that moment of crying, I was intuitively guided to the understanding that this pregnancy was many things—part of my karmic debt, a shifting of the generational lineage, exposing the Western medical field for a misdiagnoses or a lack of positivity about what is possible for our lives, completing my soul contract to never compromise my character for love, and the opportunity to share this story for a greater collective healing.

During that moment of tears, I couldn't put all this into words yet, but I intuitively knew this story was meant to help a lot of people have a greater understanding of why certain things happen(ed) for them and how to move through life's perceived unjust traumas.

My Choice

It was in that moment when I was balling that I started to pray for a miscarriage. I looked at my life twenty years ahead, and I saw this brilliant, talented, resilient, amazing woman. She was suffering, living her life for a child in a relationship dynamic she didn't want. I looked into the future, seeing myself putting my child at the center of my universe, which would have been the same generational pattern my mum had been living out within her family lineage for who knows how long. Deep down, I wasn't ready to let go of my dreams, and I wasn't willing to bring a child into this planet without my child seeing her parents very in love. I knew if I had this child, they would have seen me suffer tremendously, and I wouldn't have been the example I wanted my child to look up to.

I knew in my heart that releasing those tears was not only my karmic ties being released, it was also my mum's generational pattern and karmic debt being released. She was seeing her daughter suffer, and there was nothing she could do to help, because for so long she put me before her own happiness. That is exactly why I wound up with an unplanned pregnancy—because I was putting this guy's wants before my own, from the same generational pattern my mum taught me by putting me before her. If I would have had this child, it would have been because the child's dad wanted it, not because I wanted it, so I therefore would have passed down the generational lineage instead of healing it.

Thanksgiving passed, and it was time for me to leave Florida and fly back to California. I continued to obsessively pray for a miscarriage, even though I still hadn't confirmed I was pregnant—except for the intuitive knowing. As soon as I got home I took five pregnancy tests, and they were all positive. Then things worsened. I became afraid of the man's child that was in my stomach.

I was fearful he would want me to keep the child because he deeply desired to have children. I was afraid my life would be taken away, and I'd suffer. I was afraid he might sue me if he knew I didn't want to keep the child to gain rights over my body. These were all the thoughts running through my mind.

When I returned home, I researched clinics. I went in straight away, and they told me I had to come back in seven days. I didn't want to—I couldn't—wait that long. Every day, I felt that little baby egg growing inside me. I also felt the father's energy inside me. I was afraid to reach out to him because I just had an intuitive knowing he could easily manipulate me to keep the child. During our whole relationship, I had never stood strong in my voice, so I knew I could easily be manipulated by someone using the right tactics. It wasn't until this whole experience happened that I learned the importance of always listening to our inner guidance system and standing strong in our voice, no matter what anyone else's reaction is.

Our Inner Guidance System

This "knowing" that we have within ourselves is what I call our inner guidance system. We know not to put ourselves in certain environments that would expose our core wounds, those situations where we have not yet created strong enough boundaries. Well, my whole relationship with the child's dad I ignored my inner guidance system to get out, which is why I co-created the problem of having an unplanned pregnancy, regardless of what doctors told me.

However, in this situation, I slowed down enough to listen to my inner guidance system. I knew I could not tell the dad, otherwise I may be manipulated to keep a child I did not want, because I was not strong enough in my boundaries to say no. I truly believe we all have this inner guidance system, and, I promise you, when we slow down enough to listen to it things start to rapidly shift in our lives.

The Release of the Child

I went back to the clinic two days later, and they confirmed I was pregnant.

I screamed because of how horrific the situation was for me. I felt like the worst and ugliest and scariest monster on the planet. It was then I made my decision about what to do.

I waited outside the room for them to call me in, having extreme anxiety, including chest pain. I existed in multiple states of emotion all at once. I felt like my heart was beating outside of my chest, breaking into a million pieces, yet at the same time, I knew this was the right decision for me.

In that waiting room, a little girl started playing with me right before I was called back. We were laughing; she was maybe three years old. In an instant, I knew I was pregnant with a girl, and my daughter's soul was in the little girl's body, showing me what kind of woman she would be. I kept thinking, "Oh, my gosh, what am I doing?" But at the same time, I knew this was right for me.

As I looked into the little girl's eyes, I saw a young woman, my child, the future version of myself sitting in a clinic and making the same decision I was making right now. I knew that I would never want to bring a child into this world where she would end up in the mess I was in.

Then they called my name.

I went into the room. The clinician gave me "the pill" and I started sobbing—screaming. She said, "Colleen, are you sure you want to do this?"

I yelled, "I cannot have his baby." I threw the pill into my mouth, and I drank the whole glass of water. I threw my hands onto my face, sobbing and emitting a feeling of brokenness.

Suddenly, I knew that my whole relationship with this man was never about me; it had always been about him. For the world to capture those words from the infinite cloud and deliver them through me . . . I knew it was a message from God, letting me know I did the *right thing for me* for the first time in my life. I was no longer letting my mind, body, and soul be used for what was best for someone else's life.

I ran outside the room and I heard and saw the same little girl playing with me before I went in the room, now screaming. My daughter's soul was coming through this little girl, letting me know I was releasing the pain from my soul contract, from my own trauma, and from the soul who would have incarnated through me.

I drove home sobbing.

Tears streaming.

Lungs screaming.

Unable to look myself in the face.

During that drive home, everything changed. I imagined myself driving through a portal of hope, grace, and renewal into a new life. I saw every single person who was walking on the sidewalk differently. I saw the sun's rays hitting Earth differently. I became more present in my body. I actually felt the tear drops forming from the corner of my eye, running down my cheek, and hitting my heart.

Somehow—through divine alignment—my schedule the next day already included a planned call with my mentor and a new therapist.

Divine Alignment

Divine alignment is when things line up in our lives, as if some higher power has orchestrated events for us.

For example, when you think to yourself, "It would be really nice for $50 to randomly show up so I can buy this shirt . . . or fix my car . . . (you fill in the blank)." Then, exactly $50 randomly shows up through a check, tax return, bonus, friend's gift, or some other means, you wonder, "How in the world did I just think about this $50, and it just showed up?"

That is the co-creation of divine alignment. There is a higher power working in our favor. When this happens, it is meant to serve as confirmation that you are on the right path, so keep going. However, it is up to you to be present, to notice the many confirmations the world is sharing with you to move you in the right direction.

Trauma

The next day while meeting with my new therapist and my mentor, they could both tell I was numb. I was dissociated and avoiding what had just happened in my life.

Logically I knew what happened, yet I was protecting my heart from the trauma that had occurred. The trauma had come in multiple ways:

➤ Having an abortion
➤ Acknowledging what the medical industry says isn't always true
➤ Seeing the result of what happens from being in a relationship with a man that wasn't working for me
➤ The little girl playing with me before I went in and then screaming as I left

My head was spinning with thoughts, and they were spiraling out of control, taking me down with them.

That night I was instructed to take the second pill. I was already paralyzed with agony from the emotional pain of the first pill. Yet it was nothing like the second pill, where it felt like my stomach was being blown up . . . like an atomic bomb was going off in there.

I know the moment my angel left me. I saw a beautiful blue and green alien figure come in, grab her beautiful soul, place her in a blue, light-filled square box—like a mini galaxy—and in that moment, I found peace. I knew my daughter was safe. I knew she was going to be beside me forever.

The day after the child was out of my body, I woke up and went to a networking event. I put my best face on (because that was all I knew how to do) to take action, do something, cover it all up, and hide from my feelings. I figured when the timing was right, the feelings would come up, and I'd deal with them then. Unfortunately, this prompted me to endure more suffering, because the longer we put off dealing with the reality of our lives or the trauma we are facing, the longer we deny our feelings—the ones that are trying make us more self-aware—

the worse our lives become.

I came home from the networking event feeling happy. I felt confident with my business and a few new opportunities that arose.

Then I was hit with more trauma. After six days of pain, a time when the father and I had little to no communication, this guy called me. He told me that during the seven days we had barely spoken, he was extremely ill, including that he had been hospitalized.

Also, this was divine confirmation for me, because when I was diagnosed with cancer at age fourteen, I saw a dad yell at his wife, saying that the only reason they could not pay for their daughter's treatment was because she was a stay-at-home mom. This led me to believe my whole life that you needed money to have love and money to live, to not die. Yet, once I started to follow my dreams, I realized this was not true.

In my situation, the child's dad was unable to be there for me even if I desired for him to be there because of his health, regardless of any amount of money he may have had. This just goes to show you that money cannot buy you, your health, love, or character. The way you love stems from your character and your character can only be alive for other people to experience when you are healthy. In *An Uncompromised Life*, everything always starts by taking care of yourself, growing a relationship with your soul so that you are healthy for your character to be experienced, and then love from your heart can be felt.

As the dad of the child was sick while I was suffering, this is the perfect example of how we don't ever need to know how the laws of the universe work; instead, we should simply trust that the universe always provides harmonization to everything.

Part 2

The Beginning

When I first met the child's dad, there was a spark. I feel in love with his black squiggly eyes. It felt like there was something special about our connection from the moment I saw him—it felt familiar. This familiar feeling stems from us having known each other for centuries on end as souls from past lifetimes. At a deep level, I knew this about us. It was confirmed when he and I started getting to know each other, except I always felt something was off, which probably has to do with the massive energetic silver chains he has put to lock his heart away. I never felt fully safe to be or express myself. Yet I didn't listen to my inner guidance system that something was off, and I let my heart override my gut feelings.

We have two options when our guts tell us to avoid one thing and our hearts coax us to do it anyway. One, we can try to figure out why our gut says no and our heart says yes, which usually means we're going to experience karmic debt, completing a soul contract lesson, and ignoring the red flags our inner guidance system tries to make us aware of. Or two, we can *run* because we do not need to figure out why our gut doesn't feel safe, and we just trust our inner guidance system. This usually means we have already completed our karmic debt and soul contract lessons that would have been exposed through this person or experience. Yet, when we run from something because we trust our gut, we simply get to congratulate ourselves by saying, "Oh, I know that feeling, thank you, but no thank you." We walk away with a graceful goodbye, because we don't need to learn whatever lesson would have presented itself. Why? Because we've already learned it.

I chose option one. I didn't trust my inner guidance system. I went full force into the fire (like many of us do). Guess what happened?

Turbulence. We experienced huge miscommunication pretty early on. I was supposed to go somewhere with him, but instead, I sprinted out of his house to my car and started bawling. I cried for three hours straight, hyperventilating because I had an intuitive knowing that something was just off. Yet, for some reason, I felt like I still wanted to get to know him; I felt like there was some lesson I was meant to learn. This was a *huge* mistake because in that moment, I should have run—far away. I shouldn't have allowed a man to cause this much disturbance in my life.

The next day, I told him I was upset and shared the reason for my hurt feelings.

He said, "I don't have these types of problems in my life. You're better than this."

He had just provided *divine* confirmation, through my internal guidance system, that my gut feelings were correct, there were major red flags. I knew I needed to get out of the relationship, close the karmic debt and soul contract, start to love myself, and know a better man would be coming.

Yet . . . I still went into the fire.

The thing with soul contracts and going through karmic debt is: The pain will keep arising until we fully learn, integrate, and embody the lesson. The lessons I was missing here were numerous—having boundaries, trusting my gut, loving and honoring the beautiful person that I am, not compromising my character for love, not caring what other people think, and so many more.

A few days later, we met in person, and he shared that he wanted to get to know me (and me him) so I could understand that he would never do something to intentionally hurt me. I believed him because I had already started to trust him more than my own internal guidance system—which is a *very* dangerous place to be and live from.

After our conversation, we returned to his house, and he invited a friend over (whom we mutually knew). I knew they had some type of romantic relationship in the past, yet had no idea what the nature of their relationship was at that time.

We hung out in the pool. At one point, I asked, "Do you want kids?"

She said, "No."

And he replied, "Yes."

In that exact moment, I felt the intuitive hit, and I knew that I was the intended person the two of them desired to get pregnant. Now, whether they knew this at a conscious or subconscious level, I'll never know, and frankly, I don't care. The point of the story is that in that moment, a higher source came through me and gave me the knowledge to get out. Something did not feel right.

Do you think I listened to my intuition—to my internal guidance system?

Nope. Three months later, I was pregnant.

During those three painful and agonizing months that I had put myself through by not leaving, there were more red flags, signs, and alarm bells that went off—ones telling me to get far away from the relationship dynamic. Yet, I kept compromising my character and my internal guidance system because I still wasn't learning the lesson. Instead, I was pretending to be innocent by enjoying the "fun" moments. But honestly, not all the moments were fun for me.

During this time, I found out that this woman from the pool and him are not just friends, they lived together.

"HOLD ON! PAUSE!" I couldn't believe it. Why on earth, if they lived together, did he tell me he invited a friend over to join us in the pool? Instead, he could have said, "My partner (or the one I'm in a relationship with) lives here. She is joining us."

That misleading communication was the birth of deception for our whole relationship. That was the beginning of turning a blind eye and deaf ear to my soul—my guidance system—and what I knew to be true. I compromised my soul, making it more available for a darker power to manifest within me.

The birth of the whole relationship was distorted, and the karmic debt and lessons would keep appearing until I was ready to learn everything my beautiful soul needed to learn to evolve to the next level of consciousness. I knew intuitively what had just happened in my soul, yet I chose to just "go with the flow," which was why I ended up pregnant. It was because

I compromised my values, my character, the desires of what I wanted in a relationship, and the divinity of whom I knew I was truly meant to become to please someone else or keep them around.

Throughout this book, you'll realize just how often we do this. These are the places and circumstances where we create low-level habits, which minimize the standards of our life, despite knowing how incredible our lives can be. In this book I will teach you how to look within and do the soul work needed, so we can stop remaining victims to our own lives.

The Reveal

So, how did I end up telling the child's dad I was pregnant? While talking on the phone, I mentioned to him that I had gone to the doctor during the few days we hadn't spoken.

He asked, "Why, were you pregnant?"

I was shocked; his internal guidance system had alarmed him that I was, in fact, pregnant.

Yet, I answered, "No."

This is how our souls work. At a soul-level, he intuitively knew every detail of what had happened. I believe he consciously or subconsciously intended it the whole time, and I was a co-creator, allowing it in at a conscious or subconscious level. Yet, many of us turn a deaf ear and blind eye to what a higher power is guiding us to know. Because we have been taught and programmed by society that we must have proof in order to believe something (which is simply not true). Because when we think we need proof, we miss information coming from our souls. We must learn to trust our internal system and then the logic for everything else will drop in.

After my "No," I felt sick to my stomach. I couldn't lie. He had just called me out about what happened. I remember right in this moment, just as I write these words, a voice from God or the universe vibrating through my body that I *had* to tell him. Except I believed God kept telling me I must say it was a miscarriage; the truth was too painful, and I couldn't even admit to myself what had happened yet.

I called him back. I stood on my balcony; my hands shook. The wind slowed down to move through my face, so I felt every particle of dust enter my pores. And I said the words out loud to him.

"I cannot lie. You were right. I was pregnant, and I had a miscarriage. I was afraid to tell you, but since you guessed it, I couldn't lie."

He replied, "Oh, my gosh, are you okay?"

"Yes, it's just been very emotional."

He said, "Let me call you back."

I wasn't able to admit to myself what I had done. I was just numb. I kept trying to convince myself this was the process of a miscarriage. I was dissociating from reality and the decision I had made, because I was not ready to face all of it. I was not ready to cope with it. I still hadn't learned the lessons of what it means to live *"An Uncompromised Life."* So, I had told him only what I was willing to admit about my own reality.

A few minutes later, he called me back. "I asked you so many times if you could get pregnant and you said you couldn't."

I replied, "My doctors told me that I need to get my medication adjusted to get pregnant, and I'm not on any medication right now. I haven't been for three years." I continued, "I am not lying. I can show you research articles on this."

I felt a building rage at the medical industry for telling me a lie. Up until this point, I had not yet processed the fact that these doctors were wrong, or at worst, seemed to have lied to me. They told me I would be on medication for the rest of my life, and I have been off it since March 2017. They told me I couldn't get pregnant unless I adjusted my medication, yet I got pregnant anyway. The medical industry isn't always accurate, because the power of the human mind and our willingness to heal, will always conquer medical theory or advice. I've experienced too much proof within my own life and witnessed this happen for countless other people.

That is exactly why I am writing this book—so you can understand how to live *An Uncompromised Life,* not one based on theory, but one where you heal from your traumatic experiences without the need for a crazy-expensive therapist, anxiety medication, or needing to suffer for another day. In this book, I will reveal how to overcome any obstacles life throws at you so you can rise up and live the life you truly deserve.

On the phone with him the second time, while I was in my apartment and he was in his car in another state, I could "see" him in the quantum field pulled over in his car. I could "see" him get out of his car, and I could "hear" the wind hitting his face. I could feel our daughter running through him in the wind. This was the first time I felt his mind totally silent and still. It was the first time he was meeting her; I knew at some level he didn't have the energetic capacity to understand it all.

He then asked for space, and I did not hear from him for five days—except for the two times I quickly called him so I could find some type of comfort and relief from all the anxiety I was feeling.

Fast forward two months. He came over one night and I asked him, "Did you always know you were going to try and get me pregnant?" He said "Yes."

Again, it was at that moment, I received divine confirmation that this wasn't my karma alone. This was his karmic debt—to see how powerful his thoughts, his words, and his actions were when messing with someone else's life.

However, I was still not learning the lesson because I was needing to see a validation of comfort from him, instead of choosing to focus on healing myself. I was always more focused on him. It is never good when we allow ourselves to focus on someone else more than we focus on ourselves, because it compromises our ability to be who we are meant to be. When we think of other people before ourselves, we allow other people to come into our reality and hook into our energy, taking it for their own life force. This is the basic law of attraction for allowing unhealthy relationships to enter into our lives.

During the five days when the child's dad asked for space, I went to the movies and watched *Frozen* with another friend of mine. I could tell my friend felt that part of me was dead. I was not the happy, outgoing Colleen he was used to being around. I stared at him, feeling ice cold—much like Elsa's zap of ice in the movie. It felt like my soul had been sucked out of my body, and I had nothing left to say, be excited about, or even share. For the first time in my life I felt like a cold, empty human, whose heart had disappeared.

I suffered for the next few days, lying in my bed and crying non-stop, waiting for Ella's dad to make the phone ring. Except the phone never rang. Then, in a moment . . . everything shifted. I received a package, so I forced myself out of bed to retrieve it. I figured, "I can barely walk; I have not eaten in days. I might as well put on something nice to walk downstairs."

I slid on a pair of beautiful black pants, a pink tank top, and my new sheep-like jacket.

I went downstairs to the apartment's packages, and to my amazement, a little girl was there! She came straight up to me and asked to play. I tried not to burst out in tears.

Her mom kept suggesting they had to leave, but the little girl kept coming back to play with me.

I thought the girl was brilliant, and then I felt the soul of my child enter into this little girl's body. It was the same soul I felt from the little girl at the clinic right before I took the pill.

I asked this girl, "What is your name?"

She said, "Ella."

Then, her mom corrected her. "Sweetie, your name isn't Ella. It's Lila." At that moment, I knew my daughter's soul, and my daughter's name was Ella. It was her—my child! I ran upstairs in mixed tears of joy and pain. I fell onto my bed, knowing I had made the right decision, while knowing it was not going to be easy to move through this.

I knew God, my angels, and my soul were giving me signs and confirmations as a way for me to process my healing, walk through the trauma I had endured, and make sense out of this mess I put myself in.

Thirty minutes later, the sun set. I had a huge pink rose quartz crystal with a light in the middle of it on my kitchen island. It started to flicker on and off, on and off out of nowhere. I remembered that crystals carry souls and energy. I felt her— Ella. She was there in my crystal, letting me know she was with me, even though her dad was not.

All of a sudden, I received an intuitive hit to go downstairs and check my mail. I went down to find a pink card in my mailbox. The only information was my name, the address, and the stamped zip code from where the letter had been sent.

Envelope Mailed October 2019 Arrived December 2019

I opened it, "Holy guacamole, you're going to avo baby!" There was a picture of an avocado on it. This was ironic because Ella's dad favorite thing for breakfast was avocado toast.

I opened it, and it said, "Congratulations!!! I'm so excited for you! I hope you like these.

<3 and it had the woman's first name and last initial." Inside was $245 worth of baby-related gift cards.

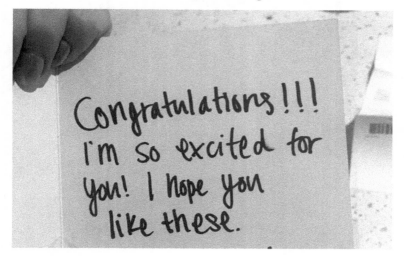

I dropped to the ground. I didn't know the person named on the card." It had somehow been mailed to my uncle's house in California, which I had just made my permanent residence, as I lived in Arizona a few months before.

I looked at the sending zip code, and it was the same city and state that Ella's dad was from. I looked up this person's name on Facebook and she and Ella's dad were Facebook friends. Plus, her Facebook profile matched the zip code on the envelope and her job title is Mother.

I almost fainted. I looked at the date the card was mailed, and it was mailed in October 2019, before I was even pregnant. I didn't know until late November that I was pregnant. I looked at one receipt, which included multiple gift cards this girl bought, and saw it was dated September 21, 2019.

I took a huge sigh, screamed, and threw my hands up in the air. How did this woman, whom I didn't know and who was connected to the man who got me pregnant, send me a pink envelope (surmising it was a girl) containing baby gift cards she bought in September, mailed in October, and it just arrived three days after I let this child go?

This is what I call a "divine plan."

This whole freaking thing had been planned without me knowing and for the highest evolution of my soul to learn the lessons I needed so I could impact the world in the way I desire. The universe, source, God, or whatever else you want to call it, was putting these confirmations in front of me, meeting Ella so I could cope with the pain, sending this impossible card, which made no logical sense, so that I knew this was bigger than just me. This whole thing wasn't about me. I didn't do anything wrong; the universe was letting me know this was part of my soul's contract and evolution, something I agreed to go through before I incarnated here as a human. I didn't need to understand why, but the universe was giving me these confirmations, so I could heal, and further my journey to impact the world.

Even though I was filled with rage, and I wanted to vomit . . . I had somehow allowed this co-created darkness into my life. . . Deep down, I knew these were all pieces to my beautiful story that would guide me to recover, thrive, and empower many other people to do the same.

My anger turned into sadness. I wanted to call Ella's dad to share this improbable situation and to find comfort—maybe even discover why this was all happening to me. Honestly, I knew that call would be taking a step backwards in my soul's evolution because he couldn't give me the answers I was seeking, and he had asked me to give him space. So I honored both him and myself. The only way I could receive those answers was by starting to have a dialogue with my soul.

Five days later, the dad messaged me that he was back in Los Angeles. He asked if I wanted to see him. I said, "Tonight would be great." He came over to my apartment and gifted me with a toy unicorn. (This will become important later in this story.)

After a nice time, I knew the moment was coming when he would leave. When he said it was time for him to go, I walked him downstairs and gave him a hug. Then, I ran into the elevator and started bawling—hyperventilating because I knew if I had kept the child, I would have always felt this way, that he would always have left me to go somewhere else or be with someone else. My heart shattered into a billion pieces because this understanding gave me divine confirmation about why I chose to not keep the baby. I would have suffered like this for my whole life, silently agonizing in the background while putting on a strong face in front of everyone. I would have given my soul to a lifestyle that routinely would have disturbed my peace.

That night, alone in my apartment, I cried and cried and cried until I passed out. I sent a prayer that I wanted it to all be better. The next morning I woke up and something was just different. The pain shifted to purpose. The trauma turned into glory. And the fear turned into love. My self-judgments and self-hate turned into empowered self-love.

I saw Ella's dad a few more times before the end of the year. On one occasion, he said, "If you were really pregnant, how much could I have paid you to keep full custody of the baby?"

I replied, "I was really pregnant, and you would have never been able to take full custody of the child."

For me, this was more divine confirmation. Remember when I took the pill, and I screamed, "I cannot have *his* baby?" I knew it was never about me; it was about him. His question here showed me that he never cared about me, he cared about extracting the value I might add to his life, which in this case would have been a baby.

I truly believe the universe doesn't want to push us to the point where someone would say such a morbid thing. The point of sharing this story is that wherever you are in your life, I want this to be a trigger, an initiation, or a wakeup call. One where you can see that if you do not feel good about a person, an environment, or a situation you are in right now, just leave. Do not stay to the point of trying to figure out why it doesn't feel good or find all the logical reasons. They may not exist, and I promise you, it will only hurt you more and take longer to get out of the energetic hole you are digging yourself in.

Ella's dad, on a human level, may have been joking. But at a soul level, every word that comes out of our little mouths matters. They serve as confirmations, signs, and symbols for us to be divinely guided in our beautiful life. Hearing him speak these words was the world giving me confirmation to get out.

Yet. I still stayed. *Why?* Because I still was avoiding the ability I had to find comfort within my own soul, instead, I was looking for comfort and answers in *him*. I have learned—and you will too—our questions can never find answers outside of us. Everything lies within us.

Deep down I was still in pain and in denial of the choice I made, even though I knew it was right for me. Except somewhere deep down inside of me I wanted him to prove me wrong—to prove that I made the wrong decision to let go of Ella. At some level, I prayed that I was the one who made the mistake. It's so funny to see how easily we place so much blame on ourselves, instead of realizing the same person who causes us pain is co-creating whatever situation we are going through.

What I desire to share for your soul, to help integrate, is this: Stop being self-critical and subconsciously trying to find all the reasons why you are wrong in life while everyone else seems to be your hero. Just stop. You are your own hero—your own savior—and no one else can get you out of the position you are in except you. Realize how many excuses you make for others' poor behaviors and recognize what you are willing to tolerate. When you're around someone, start noticing how they make you feel during the time you spend together and after. Learn to trust yourself without needing to know why things feel good or don't feel good. Just become aware of what you're feeling and move on with your life— in a way that empowers you to feel better in every moment. When you start to trust your own soul, and accept that miracles are always around you when you go within, then magic truly happens.

This leads me to another miracle I experienced in this story. Remember that unicorn keychain Ella's dad gave me when he came over to my apartment after he found out I had a "miscarriage"? Well, January, he came over again, and I looked at him and said, "What do we name her?"

He thought about it for a second and said, "El."

My heart felt like it dropped to the bottommost tip of my body. "Did you just say El, like in Ella?"

"Yes."

In my head, I said, "Oh, my gosh, Ella. She is real." This was the second confirmation from the universe that my daughter's name would have been Ella.

Then there were more confirmations having to do with crystals. The third time I hung out with Ella's dad, my selenite crystal heart spoke to me. It prompted me to give it to him. The special thing about crystals is that they carry energy and souls. When crystals are around you or someone gifts you one, it's because there is an energy within the crystal that is meant to speak with you and be with you for your soul's evolution.

This was an indication of what I already knew—we'd met in past lifetimes and I'd given him my heart numerous times. Well, I didn't think much about those crystals again . . . at least until this moment when he said the name "El."

A few days before he named the toy unicorn El, I left my apartment to get coffee, and there was a store that had a shattered window with six crystals sitting on the sidewalk. One of them was a purple amethyst heart. I thought, "Oh, my gosh! I knew it! We've had this child in previous lifetimes!" Another divine confirmation that this was from our past lives, a product of karmic debt, and a soul contract being completed.

I grabbed the crystals, and I knew I was meant to give him the purple one that was shaped like a heart. Everything was coming full circle as I remembered everything—our connections and relationship—from past lifetimes.

I chose not to say anything because I knew how crazy this all sounded. Yet it was so real to me and in alignment with the karmic debt and soul contract I was living out. Well, I gave him the purple amethyst heart crystal, and tried to explain how incredible this all was. Yet I knew he didn't really understand how miraculous and special this all was. However, I also knew in this lifetime, he maybe was not supposed to understand it all.

Deep down, I knew this was my sweet angel letting me know I was meant to own a beautiful crystal line named CrystELLA, to guide others on their journeys of remembering why they're here, empower others through their healing journeys, and educate as many people as we can to create a synchronized life filled with magic and miracles, to truly live an uncompromised life to your soul's divine mission. Part of me wanted Ella's dad to be part of this, yet part of me decided for myself that wouldn't work out well for me. Yet I kept compromising myself to be with him, until finally there came one day when I could not take it anymore.

I took him to a networking event, except we had planned to go to the beach beforehand. We ended up not being able to go because the place he dropped his car off was fifty-five minutes away from the beach, so I drove an extra two hours that day and missed the beach.

During this fiasco, he turned to me and said, "I have visions of you getting hit by a truck and going into a coma or a silver pole going through your head because of your texting and driving." My whole body froze. Energetically, I felt a huge silver pole pierce through my head. My emotional body became numb. I knew in that moment the universe was telling me that an energy was coming through this man to try and kill me.

After the networking event on the drive home, my car started to sound weird. This guy said, "What's that?"

I replied "I don't know."

He put my car in neutral while on the main road. I thought, "Oh my gosh, there is something trying to kill me through this man!" I pulled over to get gas, and afterward, as I pulled out of the gas station, a car almost hit me on the driver side—my side.

My insides screamed, "OH MY GOSH! This man's vision is trying to create my future! I need to get the heck out of my car and get away from this man!" My soul was repulsed. All the signs were there. I wanted to drive to my house as quickly as possible and get out of my car—before another car tried to hit me. So, I drove us to my house where we fell asleep. Then at midnight, this man woke me up and expected me to drive him home.

I remember I didn't want to get in my car or do this because I intuitively knew a car accident might happen.

I said, "Can't you take an Uber?" I was afraid that if I got in my car one more time that night, I was going to be in a fatal accident. My gut just knew it, and I was scared, yet I didn't have the power to use my voice.

He said, "No." No Uber. So, I got out of my bed, my heart was shaking—trembling with fear—which probably came off as anger as I started to walk to my car. Then, by the grace of God, he relented, "Fine, I'll Uber if you are that tired."

I looked up to the sky and said, "Thank You, God for saving my life." I knew that if I would've gotten into that car, something catastrophic would've happened to me.

The next day, I blocked his number and started my journey to recovery—reclaiming my relationship with my soul and forever committing to live *An Uncompromised Life*.

However, there is one final piece to this story.

I called my mum shortly after this and told her everything about this guy and about Ella.

She replied, "Do you know whose name was Ella?"

"No, who?"

"My mum's best friend; she never married and never had children."

It was the third divine confirmation that Ella is, in fact, real. I broke my mum's generational lineage, the one that said my sole purpose for existing was to be her child, I truly did save Ella, and I completed the karmic debt and soul contract with Ella's dad for my highest soul growth and evolution. These are the exact miracles that show up for you when you live *An Uncompromised Life*, which means being honest with yourself about how you are feeling and how you are acting in every part of your life. By my mum sharing this information, I knew that if I would have had the baby, it would've been this woman's soul, and I would have repeated the same generational emotional lineage. Who knows . . . if I would have told my mum everything that had happened earlier than I did, would that have been the confirmation I needed to cut ties with Ella's dad and save myself from the added trauma? Or, for me to truly live *An Uncompromised Life,* did I have to go through it all to complete my soul contract and karmic debt? Did I have to experience everything so I could come out on the other side stronger?

From this story there are so many lessons, traumas, and wisdoms birthed. As with every time something traumatic happens, wisdom and pain are born simultaneously; it's just up to you to choose to live in the trauma or the wisdom. Through my story, I shared with you how Ella was introduced to me as a real soul. Or, it could have been a way for me to cope with everything going on. I don't think the truth is something I will ever know, yet I have my truth—Ella's soul is real.

Also through this story, twelve lessons were revealed to me. Lessons about what it takes to live *An Uncompromised Life,* what it means to truly step into being an empowered woman, what it takes to shift generational lineage, what it takes to become successful in every area of your life, what it means to truly fall in love, how to surrender to the unexplainable miracles of life, and how to trust in the unknown of the universe so you can live out your fullest potential. My hope is these lessons will impact your life and your soul the way they did mine.

CHAPTER 2

Take Responsibility – You Choose This Life

You might be wondering how the heck I started to unpack and deal with this whole story I just shared with you. I had two options, like all of us do in every situation.

Option 1: We can become angry and bitter, blaming the world and everyone else for what is happening in our lives.

Option 2: We can choose to become grateful for every experience, realizing that we must take responsibility for co-creating all of our experiences in our reality (or they wouldn't be in our reality).

For example, all of us have to take responsibility for choosing to become a human. From that space, we will co-create having a loved one pass away sometime in our life, because that is part of the human experience. This relates to everything else in our lives—we must take responsibility for co-creating all of it. I believe—and from my life know to be true—that before we incarnated in this human life, we agreed to go through certain life experiences for our souls' evolution.

As I shared earlier, I know my relationship with Ella's dad and the other woman were part of completing karmic debts and soul contracts. I realized I had already agreed to go through this experience before I incarnated. Everything that occurs in our lives is something we already agreed to go through before our soul took human form. Yet, it's our responsibility to come to this awareness and turn our trauma into gifts, our pain into pleasure, and empower ourselves to become successful or remain a victim of suffering.

Once you come into agreement with yourself about taking responsibility for co-creating all experiences that have occurred (and will occur) in your life, life becomes much simpler. You no longer avoid, dissociate, lie to yourself, or cause resistance through anger, judgement, blame, or shame for everything going on.

Instead, you come into a new-found acceptance that you are responsible for your life and what has happened. You start to see how you can turn it into a story that can help you and someone else in a similar position.

I am not saying, by any means, that what you have gone through was deserved. I am simply stating that if you can find it within yourself to accept responsibility for it, that you are a soul in a human body who agreed to go through certain things in this lifetime—for your soul's evolution. Then you can shift the blame, anger, shame, and guilt away from yourself and release the resentment you carry toward other people, because whatever has happened to you was for your soul's highest evolution and growth.

Only you have the power to take responsibility, to understand that every part of your life has been co-created, and every part of your life can be healed, transformed, and used to help others, guiding you both to success.

Author Louise Hayes's book, *You Can Heal Your Life,* states that the reason cancer (or any illness) forms in the body is because of resentment. I had cancer at age fourteen because I resented the world, and I did not feel safe to express myself. Then, the world had a different form of trauma appear in my life: an unplanned pregnancy. Throughout my entire relationship with this man, I resented myself and I resented him. I resented myself for betraying my values while trying to fit into his world. I resented him because I felt like he kept asking me to do things he knew I didn't know how to say no to.

The Tangible Steps
So how did I begin to shift my life?

Step one: I decided to become responsible for this whole mess.

I got up out of bed a few days after I let Ella go, and I decided to finally look myself in the eyes in the mirror. I said, "I accept the responsibility that, through my unawareness, I co-created darkness."

As tears rolled down my face, I continued, "I forgive myself, please show me how to heal myself and others with this trauma." From that moment, a lot shifted because I declared my willingness into the universe, with an openness to move into a deeper awareness of how I could be an even brighter light in this world.

Step two: After Ella's dad told me he wanted space after what happened, I decided to call him and said, "I take responsibility for this." What I have learned is responsibility is something many of us tend to run from. Because it is much easier to look at the story I have shared and say Ella's dad is the bad guy, the truth is: he isn't. People are neutral. They are neither good nor bad until we give them meaning. Unfortunately, because of my unawareness, I co-created a dark experience that brought these features, qualities, and story out in myself. At any moment in my story, before it got to pregnancy, I could have stopped talking to him; I could have cut ties because I did not like how I was being treated, but I never did. I must take responsibility for that and understand that my inability to leave a situation I was not happy with is what guided me to co-create an unplanned pregnancy.

There were times I tried to cut things off, but I always allowed the low-level frequency of compromising my character for love back in, because my soul didn't fully learn the lesson it needed to learn. That is the thing about life: Whatever life experience is happening, there are four stages of integrating it into our being. First, it happens to us, then it happens for us, next it happens with us, and finally, it happens as us. The same lesson will come back through a person via experiences or a traumatic melt downs like I had to go through, so we can truly feel the lesson, learn the lesson, and integrate it so that we become a better version of ourselves and create the future we truly desire to live.

The reason unplanned things happen in our lives, especially the traumatic experiences that arise—financial hardships, relationship issues, or illnesses—is because we do not want to honestly look at our lives. We don't want to see our results or what is happening around us because deep down, we do not love our lives. Deep down there is something inside us that is scared, and if we actually took the time to look at the reasons why our lives are the way they are, we would have to admit that we are responsible for the chaos around us.

We must slow down, be present in our bodies, and actually look at ourselves in the mirror. Trust me, most of us avoid this more than you realize.

When you live a life where you are not taking responsibility for everything that is going on around you, the first step is admitting that deep down, you have chosen to settle for a life that is less than you deserve. You must choose to look at your life and decide to collapse everything you have known and start from scratch to create the life that you are destined to live.

This takes a huge shift. It requires gaining the courage necessary to become responsible for everything that is going on around you—no longer blaming your parents, society, your socioeconomic or income status, the inequalities in the world, relationships, or your feelings of anxiety or depression. Taking responsibility means all those excuses go out the window. I admit, it's one of the scariest things in the world, because you're left with no one to blame and no one to come save you except yourself.

In order to start taking responsibility for choosing this life, here are steps you can take:

1. Become radically honest with yourself about the reality of your life.
2. Agree that you choose everything in this life.
3. Say, "I take responsibility every time I get frustrated, angry, or off balance with my emotions," instead of saying, "He, she, they, it . . . or whatever else it is." Notice how quickly your language changes, and you are able to empower yourself through language to create a different reality.
4. Implement this practice for at least five minutes of your day. Simply sit with yourself in front of a mirror, or if you do not have a mirror, look at your phone camera or go to a shop that has a mirror. Set an intention to love and honor yourself, and then just look into your eyes for at least five minutes. Stare into your soul and see how beautiful you are; stare into your eyes and spend time getting to know yourself; and, just sit there—breathing, witnessing, and experiencing who you truly are.

This four-step practice, which you can easily implement into your life, will help you choose to take responsibility for everything that goes on around you. Even in the case of abuse, you can put a stop to the abusive behavior at any moment by being honest with yourself, telling yourself that you deserve better, and leaving to create another life. At any moment, you can change your financial state by being honest about where you are and where it is you want to go. In any moment, you can dissolve relationships that are not working, because you get to choose to take responsibility to operate at a higher frequency. At any moment, you can be in a relationship with someone and choose to take the responsibility for no longer allowing their actions to dictate your emotional state. From this space, simply watch as miracles occur as that individual shifts because they see you are no longer depending on them for emotional stability. At every moment, you can choose to take responsibility for understanding that your past trauma is not a judgment you must hold over yourself. In every moment, you can become radically honest with yourself, realizing you are the only one holding you back and you can choose to create *An Uncompromised Life*. It's a life that is true to your soul's calling—one that empowers your heart and mind to feel free because you are expressing who it is you truly are.

Through my story of Ella, I learned that when you start taking responsibility for knowing who you truly are, instead of being who everyone else wants you to be, your life shifts rapidly. You start to remember everything that makes you unique and beautiful, rather than trying to fit into a molded false perception of who you think you need to be. Once you start to remember the depth and the greatness of who you truly are, you will be excited to take responsibility because you will see what the future holds for you. I promise, it is so much greater than where you are in this moment.

This word, *responsibility*, can seem frightening. I know it was for me. On my twenty-sixth birthday, I was out to eat with someone. The exact words that came out of my mouth were, "I desire to reach that next level of success, yet that means I get to be responsible for a larger group of people, and that means I get to be solving people's bigger problems." I explained to this person that the next level of success meant I would have to constantly show up. I couldn't hide under a rock, and I couldn't pretend to be someone else. I would get to be responsible at a whole new level. When I shared this, I had a deep fear that once I did become responsible for myself or even for more people at a deeper level, that I would not be happy.

The irony was that I was not happy being irresponsible—sharing my body, my heart, and my mind with a man who was offering me a situation I was never going to feel good about. I was avoiding responsibility, allowing myself to "go with the flow" because I thought it would be easier than saying my truth. Obviously, that didn't work out for me very well, and if you are reading this, I'm guessing it's not working out too well for you either.

The question to come back to is: *Are you willing to be honest with yourself for the subconscious and/or conscious habits you have chosen to create—the ones in which you are lacking responsibility for being who you truly are?*

Speaker and author Abraham Hicks says it beautifully, "A belief is just a thought we keep having over and over again."

We have tens of thousands of thoughts every day, some conscious and others unconscious, and it's in our unawareness of the thoughts we have that we co-create darkness or situations we do not want into our reality.

For some reason, I created a subconscious belief that more responsibility meant less happiness. I think many of us do this. When we take time to sit with ourselves and truly learn who we are, how we operate, and what type of impact we want to leave in this world, we will come to learn that more responsibility means more fun. The responsibilities you have right at this moment, until you choose to become aware, are responsibilities from your children, your job, your friends, or even your own mindset. You get to stop and ask yourself, "Are these responsibilities the ones I really want to have and are they empowering me to feel good?" In essence, are you living and embodying the responsibilities that your soul desires for you or for what everyone else wants from you?

When you look into your eyes are you fulfilling daily tasks and habits that set your soul on fire? When you start to practice looking in your eyes over a period of time, you get to know who you truly are. You realize that you have a specific purpose that you are meant to live on this planet. You then have a responsibility to share who it is you really are with every single person you meet. Because you are not here to play small and you are not here to keep to yourself—you are here to do big things that matter.

This all starts with shifting your mindset to see that the more responsibility you have, the more fun your life will be.

The more responsibility you have, the more exciting your life will be. The more responsibility you have doing the things you love, the more things will naturally flow with new people who will be created into your beautiful reality.

Responsibility can seem scary—it can be something you hide from or it can be invigorating. The first step is realizing you are responsible for the way your life is right now. The second step is realizing you can change your responsibilities and create responsibilities you love instead of mindlessly completing tasks because you think you have no other options.

The reality is *you always have choice*. You get to take responsibility that you alone created everything that exists around you, and you get to choose again to create something even more beautiful, if you desire. You have the choice to create a life that is uncompromised. *An Uncompromised Life* doesn't happen by accident; it happens by choice. *An Uncompromised Life* happens when you take the responsibility for accepting where you are now and choosing where you are destined to go.

So ask yourself:

➤ What am I choosing at this moment?

➤ Am I choosing my soul's truth?

➤ Am I choosing to be that human that I see when I look into my own eyes to meet my own soul?

➤ Am I choosing to create responsibilities that feel good for me?

So, lesson number one is become responsible to be honest with yourself that you have the power to choose this life, because if you are not being honest with yourself, the world cannot give you honest opportunities that will transform your life so you can live *An Uncompromised Life*—a life indicative of your soul's true purpose, calling, and desires.

CHAPTER 3

Understanding the Natural Laws of the Universe

started this book within fifteen minutes of my biggest life challenge to date. I have coached hundreds of clients, written multiple books, and offered advice to all my friends, yet deep down, in a tiny little box hidden in my heart for safekeeping, I had hidden myself. I had numbed myself to everything. I would look in the mirror and feel nothing; I would take a shower and feel nothing; I'd wake up in the morning and feel nothing. I'd be with people around me who loved and adored me, and I would feel nothing. People would cry tears of gratitude around me, telling me how inspiring or how amazing I am, how I have changed their lives, and I would feel nothing.

Not a single thing.

People would tell me they loved me, and I'd wonder, "How on earth could you love someone like me?" I have since learned many of us walk through life that way.

All of these thoughts, all of this numbness, and the lack of feeling anything in the world ends up compounding until it blows up in your face and in multiple areas of your life. Your finances, your confidence, your mindset, your relationships, your business—everything you care deeply about—can change in an instant when you choose to compromise the value and heart of your soul. You can keep pretending and you can keep hiding, yet while you are doing this your body, your mind, and your soul are keeping score, and the consequences will catch up to you.

Lesson two (understanding the natural laws of the universe) started for me with something I learned from a mentor as she taught me how to change my relationship with money. To do so, I'd have to learn how to have a more intimate relationship with it. This mentor suggested that I start everyday by looking at my bank account. So I did that, and I'd fill out an Excel spreadsheet of what came in, and I'd set aside ten percent for my savings account. Then, I'd look at my expenses. There came a point where I'd see the number of my expenses growing and growing, yet I'd feel nothing.

No emotion, not even fear. If we have no emotion about money, then we might not be making very much. Because emotions are what allow us to feel excitement to start creating and building in the world. It is from this place of excitement we began to act from alignment—creating and building to our soul's calling—that money begins to flow easily and endlessly to us.

I was showing up to do this exercise my mentor shared so I could improve my relationship with money. Yet, overtime I'd see the growing expenses without experiencing the emotions of happiness or stress. I just had a knowing within me that at some time, the debt would change to a profit. I looked at my money like this every day for months, just knowing the numbers would change, even though I had no idea what to do in order to start the process. I invested in tons of online programs, I studied all my income and expenditures, I tried to create opportunities for my business, yet it all felt forced. I had no actual emotion of excitement or feelings running through me. This generated no real results because the universe operates on energy and frequency, not logic.

What is Energy?

I've mentioned energy through the book, but let's dive in fully. When you type energy into Google, you'll discover that energy is the ability to do work; to create momentum for how things change and move. Understanding energy, what it is and how it works, is an important universal law each of us should understand. At a scientific level, everything can be measured in Hz frequency. Everything that is created in our world is simply feedback in the form of energy, based on a frequency at which we vibrate.

If you are suffering from trauma, it is because you are vibrating at the frequency of trauma. If you are attracting emotionally unavailable people, it is because you are vibrating at the frequency of emotional unavailability. If you are struggling with finances, it is because at some level, you do not believe you are worthy of living in abundance, so you are vibrating subconsciously at that frequency.

Every single thing in your life is just feedback from those vibrations. Here's a question to ask yourself, "What do you really desire in life right now?"

Whatever it is you deeply desire to have in your life right now, it will not become your reality if you are not matching the energy the universe requires for you to receive what you desire. The universe will provide you with feedback through perceived problem frequencies that it wants you to focus on. For example, if your deepest desire is to make more money, yet the money isn't coming it's because the universe wants you to focus on how you can help others, not the money. Because money is simply an exchange of you offering a solution for someone's problems and being paid for it. If it is coming to you in health, the world wants you to focus on the emotions you are suppressing or avoiding. If it comes to you in relationships, the universe is wanting you to focus on boundaries, standards, and self-love. If your largest perceived desire in life is not happening right now, it is likely coming to you through a perceived problem the universe needs you to focus on enhancing instead of ignoring, before the universe gives you your perceived deepest desire. From my experience, the laws of the universe are always speaking to you in this manner—where your perceived problems are simply an opportunity to realign yourself to feeling good, so you then become available for the universe to deliver your deepest desires.

Another way to say this is: Everything you already desire is available to you within the universe—all your desires and wishes can come true right now. However, the reason your desires aren't coming true is because something is out of alignment in your energy field. The way the universe communicates this to you is either through not delivering your biggest desire or by offering a pain point for you to look at.

For example, with me, I really desired to make a million dollars before I became pregnant because to me, I thought that was success. Well I was creating debt in my life. That debt was energetic feedback from the natural laws of the universe not giving me my greatest desires. Just because I had not yet seen that money didn't mean I wouldn't have success. Rather, I needed to learn that helping other people is the success. I was not accepting the message of where my focus should have been shifting, either. I just kept spending way more than normal, knowing there would eventually be a problem if something did not change. When I spoke with my soul, I knew deep down in me that something would change, and I would eventually get the idea—find understanding. Eventually I would get the inspiration and motivation to follow through on a commitment I made to myself to feel an emotion when spending my money.

Yet this idea of something changing "someday" leads to living a compromised life. Because when we choose to think "someday" something will change, that leads to spending our time doing mindless activities, just so we avoid looking at ourselves. For example, I knew I was overspending, yet I would still spend money on pointless coaching programs, clothes, makeup, and other things that I thought would make me feel beautiful. Instead, I ended up in more debt, feeling more unsure of myself, and disturbed about how this was all going to work out.

Remember, the universe only responds in energy—I was vibrating at an energetic level of greed, self-serving ideology, and the idea that success was measured with a dollar amount. I was not listening to the energetic frequency of the universe. Well, it decided to send me a larger energetic frequency instead of just debt to respond to my unawareness and resistance to looking at my own life, which was allowing me to become pregnant.

This pregnancy stopped me dead in my tracks because it was not what I wanted for my life at that moment. I had no option except to start looking at what frequency I was vibrating at for this to come into my reality, regardless of what doctors diagnosed or recommended.

Don't get this confused with the universe sending us these life events as a way to punish us. These things are sent to empower us to wake up and say, "OH, my life is meant to become better." These perceived problems are meant to get us vibrating in new frequencies where we start to pose these questions:

> How did I get so out of alignment that this became my reality?

> How did I end up so far away from allowing the universe to flow through me?

Ideally, our answers will bring us back into flow with the natural laws of the universe. We can discover how to co-create with the universe instead of resisting it. We can answer the question, "What am I supposed to be looking at in my life that I can upgrade so I don't keep repeating the same patterns?"

With all these answers, we move into a new place—one where we often find out that our biggest desire was actually a distraction. The biggest desire we had been choosing to focus on was actually allowing us to compromise ourselves and our character in order to obtain that desire. This goes against the laws of the universe. I thought my desire was a million dollars, yet my real desire was to feel a connection with myself and those around me. I thought that the more money I made, the more I would feel I was impacting others. It was not until I realized that impacting others starts in this present moment, by impacting my own life. That this holds the key for me to live *An Uncompromised Life,* so I can impact others too. It was never about my desire to make money; it was always about my desire to connect with myself, yet that desire was masked by money. Take a moment to feel into where you can apply how you mask an emotional issue with a tactical problem.

Deep down, I knew everything I am sharing with you in theory, yet I kept reaching for that million dollars. It wasn't until after I became pregnant that I honored the connection within myself, by understanding how powerful it is to feel a little egg growing inside of me. I'll never forget the moments; I could feel that little egg moving around inside of me. When

I was at yoga, I could feel it. When I was lying in bed, I could feel this extra energy buzzing inside of me. The natural laws of the universe wanted me to understand how powerful the frequency of connecting to myself truly is, which is another reason I believe I became pregnant. I believe the natural laws of the universe want you to understand that, too—that you already have more than enough to start connecting with yourself and creating the life you desire right now.

The laws of the universe desire for you to be living in the fullest expression of who you are, so you feel whole and complete right now. This place of practicing and aligning yourself to your true desires allows them to show up as a natural effect of universal law, without you having to push, suffer, or even take real action to make it happen. It's already waiting for you and has been the whole time, but your focus was on everything else. Just like becoming pregnant was always available for me, and I chose to focus on believing the medical doctors, instead of trusting that it could be possible. It's time to accept and join the flow of frequencies available to you now.

In order to master the laws of the universe, the alignment is to allow you to be in such a place where in every moment, you are being true to who you really are—practice connecting with your body, not your mind. Now, you may be asking, "How do I practice being in my body, not my mind?"

Here are few different signs that you are living in your head, not your body:

➤ If you sit down to have a conversation with people, and you struggle to look them in the eyes

➤ If you are expressing yourself, and you move your body and head around a lot because you are trying to bypass feeling the emotions that align with the words you are saying

➤ If you struggle to stay focused on one task at hand for a long time because your mind starts wandering and daydreaming about a possible future reality that may or may not exist

➤ If you are someone who repeats the same story over and over to multiple friends to gather data on what they think, so you can sit and ponder some more about what may or may not happen in a future reality

➤ If you hate being around lots of people, not wanting to say anything out loud because you assume people already know everything they should about you

➤ If you create a reality about people in your head, assuming they all know where you stand on every issue

These are all examples of living in your head, and they can cause you to live a compromised life—one that goes against who you truly are, because you are working against the laws of the universe. The universe desires for us to flow with life, the universe desires for life to feel good, the universe wants us to receive all of our desires forevermore. However, when we live in our head, it takes us out of the present moment, and we can't feel everything we have available to us right now. The natural laws of the universe respond to us in a frequency of us being inside of our heads, not our bodies. And our emotions come from our heart which is in our body, not our mind.

Here is an example: I was madly in love with this man when I worked for a corporate job in Houston, Texas. I had a great friend who was also a co-worker, and we sat in the same cubical. I would talk her ear off about how I felt about this man, including all our breaking up and getting back together. I would "thought process dump" and share all my emotions with this friend of mine. However, whenever I talked with the guy whom I was madly in love with, I had no emotions to share; I had no thoughts to share because I just wanted to enjoy the bliss and the good parts of the relationship. I did not want my time with him to be consumed with my deepest thoughts and feelings that were actually coming through me and about us. This containment of my feelings from him led to me living an extremely compromised relationship.

Why?

I was never sharing what was actually going on in my head or my heart with him. I was compromising my true feelings and thoughts in exchange for a moment of pleasure or even just to lie there, having a moment of physical touch that seemed like love in the moment. However, when I was not around him, I was so in my head about everything that the universe kept showing me—allowing this guy to do things that would hurt me, make me unhappy, or feel unloved or unappreciated. The laws of the universe were responding to my frequency of being in my head when I was not around him, yet when I was with him, I believed I was simply living in bliss. The universe was speaking to me though pain to let me know I was going in the wrong direction. We are not meant to live in this addictive loop of instant short-term pleasure. Instead, we can live for the long-term, creating emotionally healthy choices.

Awareness of Frequencies

So how do we become aware of the universe speaking to us based on the frequency we are operating at?

There are a list of things you can do to become aware of frequencies. The first thing is to be willing to honestly look at yourself, your life, and your relationships and ask, "Am I really expressing what is important to me right now?" I know many times, based on both this relationship and the one with Ella's dad, I did not express my feelings on how I was doing, or what was happening for me in the moment. It took four years of experiences like this, compounding over time, for the universe to respond and for me to become pregnant. The universe was working in the frequency of me ignoring the signs it was offering me that I was in pain; I was living in my head and not happy. It took me becoming pregnant for me to finally receive the gift and understand the lessons I needed to learn to integrate into my life forever.

This leads me to a question for you.

Are you truly happy in your life right now?

And even if you are happy, the question becomes, "Is there more happiness available for you?"

The answer is almost always *yes, there is.*

You can always grow your happiness by starting to believe you can help people enhance their lives. Ultimately, helping others will empower you to become aware of a larger happiness frequency you have available for you—to live a life beyond what you can even imagine in this moment.

Once we start to become aware that everything that occurs is frequency and everything around us happens as feedback from the natural universal laws on where we are vibrating at, then we can ask, "How can I become more aware of subconscious, compromised behaviors and move them into uncompromised thoughts, feelings, and behaviors so I enhance my life experiences?"

It's a big question to answer. From this position of acknowledging the natural laws of the universe and starting to integrate yourself with the frequency instead of subconsciously being unaware, your life begins to shift. You get to be radically honest with yourself about the thoughts and feelings going on inside your head and body. Then you get to communicate them in a way that feels good for you and feels good for other people who hear you. Once you start to become aware of your thoughts and feelings and take responsibility for being the one that has those thoughts and feelings, you will feel better about communicating them. When you feel good about communicating them, other people usually start to feel good about hearing you communicate your feelings.

When you are living life in a compromised way, you are consciously or subconsciously choosing to ignore the signs the universe is giving you. I promise you, every answer to every question you have is written in huge black and white letters in your life. Natural universal law allows the universe to speak to you in energetic vibrations through people, situations, money, relationships, trauma, and family. If you feel confused or unsure of why something is happening, I would suggest this means that the thoughts and feelings you are having aren't allowing you to move in the divine flow and order of the universe.

As I suggested before, you may be walking through life feeling numb, as I was with my money—numb to how you put on clothes, numb to how you brush your teeth, numb to the words that are coming out of your mouth, and even numb to how amazing the sunshine feels on your face. When you are living life compromised, you are numb, unaware of the patterns, thoughts, feelings, and behaviors you are living out. Once you start to become aware of the thoughts and feelings you are having, you get to start transforming them.

Here is a simple example from daily life: You are not happy while cleaning the house, yet you are doing it anyway. As you clean, you are not communicating (out loud) to anyone those thoughts in your own mind—you hate cleaning the house. Well, this feeling of entrapment about cleaning is going to cause a build-up of resentment. Over time, you'll end up lashing out in another area of your life—through shopping, eating, drinking, or the avoidance of bigger problems. So the best thing to do is become aware of how much you hate cleaning the house, accept it, and admit to others that you hate cleaning the house. Then choose to allow the laws of the universe to show up and support you in finding a solution.

At that point, you can stop doing something you hate and allow yourself to hear the answers flowing through you. "How can I transform doing something I hate and instead fill this time with something that feeds my soul?"

The universe will allow ideas to start flowing through you instead of you being stuck in the energy of "I hate doing this, but I have to do it." Ideas, such as hiring a cleaning person, adding it to your kids' chores, or asking your nieces or nephews or a friend's kid if they are wanting to make some extra money.

Do you see how these thoughts were always available to you? The laws of the universe mean there are infinite, never-ending frequencies that are available to you which you can (and should) expand your life with. If you are vibrating at the frequency that says, "I must suffer and figure this all out alone," then new ideas to upgrade your life cannot come through you. In these moments of negative thinking and forcing yourself to do things you hate, the universe is asking you to slow down and simply ask the question, "Is there a better frequency I could be operating out of?"

Now, if you are reading this book and instead of saying, "Yes, I can hire my nephew, or that neighbor," your mind straight away thinks, "I don't have the money for a cleaning person" or "my roommate (or partner) will never split this with me," those responses prove my point. The laws of the universe are responding to your suffering because you are putting it out into the world that nothing can change, instead of seeing creative possibilities available to you.

We were created to discover possibilities, be creative, and speak the thoughts and things that feel good, so we can create solutions with the universe, but it's up to you to choose that reality for yourself.

Relationships and the Laws of the Universe

Let's talk specifically about relationships and the laws of the universe. If you are unhappy, have you taken the time to sit down and figure out why you are not happy with the way a certain relationship is going? Have you communicated to yourself effectively about what your needs are within a relationship and if they are being met? Have you ever sat down and truly realized you are not happy? Or are you just forcing yourself to relive a relationship dynamic over and over again, hoping it will bring a different result somehow? Are you watching movies, daydreaming, or talking excessively to your work friends about why you're not happy, yet doing nothing, such as having a conversation with the other person you're in the relationship with?

It's important to become aware of the thoughts, feelings, and behaviors you are living with in your life. Without this self-dialogue, self-awareness, and conversations with people you have relationships with, change will be hindered.

➤ Are there short-term pleasures that you're allowing that may be hindering your long-term desires of living *An Uncompromised Life*?

➤ Are you being true to who you are in every moment?

If not, the universe will respond and your income levels may not be where you want them to be, your relationships may suffer, your friendships may fall apart, your adventures may disappear, and so on.

Whereas the moment you say, "Okay, I am not happy, and something in my life is not working. Where am I forcing something instead of going with the natural flow of the universe?" You'll start to see changes.

Different questions allow you to receive different frequencies of what is available for you—frequencies you couldn't see before because you were operating out of the previous energetic space you were in.

For example, if you're having relationship problems you start asking specifics, such as:

➤ What needs are not being met?

➤ Do you need to have a dinner date once a week together?

➤ Do you need to pray together in the morning?

➤ Do you desire random texts throughout the day when he thinks of you?

➤ Do you need to work out together?

Clearly say what it is you feel is missing in the relationship and provide a solution to what you are desiring to create more of. Another thing within a relationship dynamic is you can start to see where you are missing giving yourself some of the things you desire. Are you blaming your partner for not paying attention to you when you should be giving attention to you? Instead of your partner telling you you're beautiful, you could remind yourself that you're beautiful. Then you may start to see how your partner ends up surprising you by saying the things you want to hear because you started to say and embody them yourself. You shifted your thoughts from anger, blame, and shame to empowerment, confidence, and excitement.

These are the small thoughts, communication avenues, and behavior patterns we get to change so we move *with* the laws of the universe, instead of against them. This can be perceived as a challenging lesson to master, but I promise it's very simple. It's choosing to be true to you in the small moments, so you avoid having to go through something catastrophic like I did with Ella. Even if you did have a traumatic experience, it's understanding that instead of resisting the trauma, how you can work with the frequencies of the universe to make the trauma happen for you and for others' journeys.

Think about it, if I had not gone through what I went through with Ella, I would have never written this book, and I'm not sure I would have recovered and rebounded so quickly. I would have still been resisting the laws of the universe, staying stuck in this experience because it is usually perceived as negative. Instead, I allowed the flow of the universe to release this back into the world in a beautiful heart-centered way to guide others through their own self-healing journeys. Since I believe in the laws of the universe and taking anything life throws at us and turning it into a greater collective healing for myself and others, I found the courage to communicate my story in such a way that I am not a victim, but rather empowered and proud of the work I have done to allow such a beautiful story to come out of such a perceived morbid topic. It's in taking that exact action which leads to compounding effects of the natural laws of the universe that delivers you frequencies resulting in you living *An Uncompromised Life.*

It's when you practice this in the small moments of becoming aware of what you are truly thinking and feeling, and communicating them in an expansive way—not as a victim—that the natural laws of the universe can flow through you to co-create solutions that shift your reality to be greater than you ever imagined. This process doesn't need to take years; it just takes practice on a moment to moment basis, which then ends up compounding into days, weeks, years, and even lifetimes—living true to yourself instead of compromising who you are. You shouldn't allow yourself to live a life that was not meant for your destiny. When you have mastered the laws of the universe by only responding and playing with the frequencies around you, then you can expand the infinite frequencies available for you. In that journey is your greatest healing, happiness, wholeness, and love, which you might not be able to imagine in this moment—because it is just that magical.

CHAPTER 4

The Dis-ease of People Pleasing

Lesson three answers the question, "Why do awful, heart-breaking, and traumatic things happen in our lives?"

If you are anything like me, you have spent most of your life pleasing people, doing everything you can to get to the top, proving your worth, or compromising your soul's true nature because you are living in fear of being true to you. You are at dis-ease. You were taught, even if indirectly, that if you were more committed to being who you are instead of pleasing everyone else around you that you were selfish. If others weren't happy with you, you wouldn't create success, and you may not have any friends.

Something my mum always told me was to be quiet and listen. I was always meant to follow the rules, and if I broke them, I was always grounded or sent to my room. From a young age, I was trained to please my parents . . . or else I would be put into isolation. On top of this, my parents were lawyers, so from the beginning I learned that if you do something wrong you might be breaking the law, which instated a lot of fear in me. This ended up costing me opportunities to believe I could obtain a state of peace and help a lot of people by being myself instead of working in a corporate job. I even forced myself to be around people who were making me question my sanity because it seemed better to go with the flow than to follow what I knew to be true for me in my body.

I believe we are all born with a knowing of what is best for us. Yet, around age thirteen, children already have it ingrained in them to either be more committed to being themselves or having the dis-ease of people pleasing. (It's dis-ease because when you are uneasy about something it usually ends up causing an emotional or physical disease). It all goes back to how our parents, teachers, or the leaders we admire taught us to be, which again, isn't necessarily their fault because many times, they didn't know any better. This is why I always say, "In our unawareness, darkness is co-created."

People say America is "the land of the free." As I've traveled to over forty countries, lived in five countries and five states in the U.S.A., what I know to be true is that freedom doesn't exist for everyone. We are influenced by our environments. Some of us live in an environment where we are taught to please people or not to share our feelings. We are taught that we must suck it up, and do things we don't want to do.

Guess what? We grow up to be adults who go to parties that we don't want to go to, take jobs we don't want to take, and hang out with friends whom we don't want to be around.

Why?

Because we were told from a young age that freedom couldn't exist for us, that we must do certain things before we can even think about being ourselves. We may live in an externally so called "free" world, yet when we sacrifice our wellbeing to please our parents, jobs, or the government, we are not free. We have allowed ourselves to become trained and conditioned to please others, which creates dis-ease in our lives and eventually disease through health, finances, and relationships.

As teenagers we start to build the foundations of our lives and careers, and many times the foundations are based on uneasiness—pleasing other people instead of doing what we know to be true for ourselves. We think about money and how success is going to work out before we think about what feels good for us—things we'd love to work at for forty years. The truth is that from an early age, we already have a pretty good idea of what it is we want to do in life, what we know to be right for us, and what is certainly wrong for us. Yet, we get sidetracked and sometimes we end up doing jobs we hate in our efforts to please other people over ourselves.

From a young age, I was trained and programmed to compromise who I was to make my parents proud so I could feel love and validation from them instead of knowing how to trust my own inner guidance system when it told me something was not good for me. This leads to the creation of a lifetime of habits regularly compromising who we are because we think if we please other people, we will finally feel whole, complete, and at peace.

For example, when I was in high school, my parents wanted me to go through an International Baccalaureate Program, and I knew deep down it was not right for me. It was the same twelve people in every single class for two years. I knew the people who were in the class, I knew this particular program was set up for people who wanted to be doctors or lawyers—which was not me—and I knew there was only one teacher whom I really liked. I told my parents I would try it anyway. I wanted to please them and make them happy by doing something new. However, you can probably guess what happened—I HATED it.

It made me very sick. I stopped doing sports. And I started drinking and partying more. I was trying to please my parents at age sixteen, instead of following a more creative path—one that would have actually been better for me to start at that age.

Once we become aware that we formed a subconscious habit from a young age, where we have more loyalty to pleasing other people than ourselves, we can start to shift the habit and move into living *An Uncompromised Life*.

From a young age, it was reinforced through both my parents that it's important to do what they say because they know what is best for me. The reality is no one knows what is best for you besides you. That is why, as parents, it's important to refrain from telling our kids what to do, and instead, have an open dialogue with them about why they are feeling angry, why they are distant, and even why they want to watch television instead of having dinner with us. The conversation needs to shift at a young age to *why* are you feeling this way?

Even as adults, in our friend-to-friend conversations, we shouldn't shame our friends if they are not doing well or there is something going wrong. Instead, our goal is to become a guide by asking questions so people can come to their own awareness about how they are *forcing* themselves to do things to please others instead of being true to who they really want to be.

To this day, I will call my mum and tell her about alien landings, or that COVID-19 was a man-made virus, or that some government is corrupt based on research I found from my academia world, and she will still say, "That is fine to say it to me; don't say it to anyone else."

I think to myself, "I am twenty-six years old, and this woman still thinks some crazy, fantasy army is going to come after me for speaking my truth in a conversation with some random person, when that just simply is not the case."

This is why it is important to understand generational lineage. It's not my mum's fault that she says this; she just doesn't know any better, and she is acting out of programming in love and care because she doesn't want anything bad to happen to me. The reality in her head is that she believes people might kill me if I say my truth. However, to remain true to myself instead of pleasing her by telling her I am not going to say anything, I respond to her by saying, "Great. I am going to say it, and she will just find out that I've said it publicly anyway."

I don't argue or get into a long conversation or debate; nor do I tell her I am going to continue to say it. I just thank her and move along with the conversation because I realized long ago it's the best way to stop allowing our parents' programming or even their parents' programming to impact us. When we argue, we compromise the field to cause tension and anger, and it removes us from authentic connection. It's better to simply listen, receive it, and through your own actions, become more committed to being true to you. Because that is when results show up and you become the living example to show your lineage that living *An Uncompromised Life* is possible. Otherwise when you do things to please those around you, you are suppressing yourself and sourcing your love from false and invalidating relationships. This is what I've learned with my mum and Ella's dad.

For my entire life, both of my parents deep down felt their purpose was to be parents. I'm not saying this is bad. Yet, they didn't really know how to deal with a creative, colorful daughter because they were both very logical with black-and-white thinking from the programming their parents had given them.

They always thought they would know what was best for me before I knew what was best for me, which was just not the case.

At times, did they know hanging out with certain friends was not good for me?

Yes.

Did they know that I was meant to get a college education?

Yes.

Yet, when I wanted to watch television instead of having dinner with them, was that what was best for me?

No.

When I wanted to be up on my computer instant messaging people instead of hanging out with them, was that what was best for me?

No.

They didn't know how to get me in a place to communicate as a child. They didn't know how to ask me why I was angry, why I wanted to be myself, or why I didn't feel like I related to other children in school. They didn't have the emotional training or awareness to understand how to help me, just like most parents don't. They were doing the best they could with the knowledge they had, which was good enough. Remember, I chose to go through that before I incarnated in my body, for lessons that my soul needed to go through.

Remember, everyone is operating within the system they learned from childhood, which is why always being a student to further educate ourselves is so important. We can aim to improve our awareness instead of acting in unawareness, which co-creates darkness. I learned from my parents that I needed to do what would make them happy, even if it didn't make me happy, because that was the only way to get the things I wanted. Then, I sought out relationships in which I would make other people happy before myself—to get what I thought I needed and wanted. This is *not* a way to live. Most of us don't even realize we are more committed to pleasing people than we are committed to pleasing ourselves; that is the problem. Think about it. How often do you do something for a friend because you "should" do it, and then, you end up angry or resenting that friend? These types of moments compound over time and result in something like a traumatic event (like having an unplanned pregnancy with Ella). It's only at this point that many of us wake up to see that something needs to change. Yet in reality:

> We are worthy of feeling good now.
> We are worthy of pleasing ourselves first.
> We are allowed to be selfish in order to be selfless.
> We are allowed to say *no*.
> We do not need to give explanations of why we don't want to do something.

Here is an example: One day, I was driving in my car on the way to my apartment and Ella's dad asked me, "Are you sure you're not on medication?"

I was in shock and replied, "NO! Are you?"

However, the problem wasn't that Ella's dad asked me this question. The problem was that I allowed myself to get into an environment where I was driving someone to my house who had the ability to ask me this question. I was more committed to how other people viewed me than I was to treating myself with love and kindness. Because if we understood how brilliant, magical, and miraculous we all are, there is no way we would ever allow someone to speak to us this way, continue to drive them to our home, and let them sleep in our bed.

There was another time when I opened my fridge and realized I had more in my fridge for the people who came over to visit than I did for myself. I had others' favorite drinks, and I didn't even have my favorite drink. I bought liquor for others, and I don't even drink liquor.

I wonder if you can you relate to this?

We get someone else a gift, and we never gift ourselves with something. We go grocery shopping and get our kids and spouses everything they want and forget to buy ourselves what we wanted. We plan everyone else's outfits for the family picture, but forget to buy ourselves new clothes for it.

The reality is that at some point in our lives, we have to take a look at ourselves in the mirror and say, "I am worthy of pleasing myself more than I please others." There has to be a point when you decide to choose *you*. For me, that point came with me having to let go of Ella all alone—with no real support—because I knew the dad would have wanted me to keep her.

I hope through this book you do not have to come to such a place in your life where choosing you means having to let go of your child. Over time, I chose to let my people pleasing DIS-ease get to the point where I was settling for such uneasiness that giving me the disease of an unplanned and unwanted pregnancy was the only wakeup call God could send me for me to start choosing me. I decided from that moment on that I would birth this beautiful book to educate, empower, and activate more people to see that we get to choose everything.

We chose to have every experience; we chose to be around certain people; and we chose to live this life we have. At every moment, we can decide to choose again, putting ourselves first. Just know that in every choice, there is a lesson. In every hardship, wisdom is birthed, and in every moment, there is a chance for you to rewrite your script. However, you must choose it for yourself—not for someone else in hopes they will like you, because that results in you being the doormat that people step on as they expand their lives while you stay stagnate.

The sad truth is many people live their whole lives unconsciously hoping and desiring to be saved. There were moments throughout my life when I was hoping to be saved, and there were times I was saved. When I was diagnosed with cancer at age fourteen, the doctors saved me. When I was too drunk in college, friends saved me. When I turned an assignment in late in school, teachers saved me because I was usually a good student.

But then came Ella. She was a decision no one could save me from except myself. There was no doctor, no magic wish, and no redo button. I had ignored all the red flags and signs to end this relationship. I was faced with the result of living into the dis-ease of people pleasing, putting this man before my own needs and desires, which allowed a baby I did not want from this relationship to be conceived in my stomach.

This was my defining moment. Would I overcome the disease of people pleasing and choose myself? Or would I surrender again, allowing this guy to use my mind, heart, and body to fulfill his needs before my own?

In letting Ella go, I chose me. It birthed a newfound relationship with my soul and my calling in life—to guide as many people as possible to the realization that you do not have to live a compromised life. Your life does not have to hit rock bottom. Your life does not have to be a roller coaster of emotions. Your life can be filled with grace. Your life can be filled with hope. Your life can be filled with a beautiful relationship with yourself first, before anyone else, which opens the door to receiving miracles and magic.

To become aware of the dis-ease of people pleasing and understand how to release it, you must slow down enough to see that you have a soul. You have gut instincts, and you have real feelings. These gut instincts and feelings were present when you were a young child. They still exist underneath all the crap you have put on top to cover them up. At some point, you became more committed to trusting others' opinions, as if they knew what was best for you. Come back to having a relationship with your soul and heart in every moment, and this will dissolve the dis-ease of people pleasing.

When you choose to have a conscious relationship with your soul, it's truly the only savior that can save your life. I know this because of my soul; my soul is what saved me from dealing with the pain of losing Ella. To start pleasing yourself, you must find ways to feel fulfilled internally when you realize there is nothing left outside of you that can help the numbness you are feeling.

I remember feeling numb for days. I remember being so in my head with the racing thoughts about how everything was going to work out. I remember wanting validation from Ella's dad. I wanted validation from God. I wanted anything, so I didn't feel the numbing pain of letting go of the child inside of me.

I started to talk to my soul in a way I never did before. I just started by saying (out loud), "Hi, show me how to love you." From that moment, my whole life changed because my soul co-created and guided me to save myself. My soul empowered me to start receiving instead of constantly doing things to prove my worth to the world. This relationship with my soul is what guided me to get out of bed when I was crying. My relationship with my soul is what told me to sleep when I wanted to work. My relationship with my soul is what pushed me to do yoga instead of phone a friend. My relationship with my soul is what gave me strength to finally let go of Ella's dad since she would help me heal in ways he could not. This relationship with my soul is what gave me strength to write this book, be vulnerable, and know that none of this is about me. Most people wait, like I did, till they're just about at rock bottom with nothing left inside before give themselves the gift of Self. My hope is that you start today. Talk with your soul and be more committed to her than giving yourself away to everyone else around you, leaving nothing left for you.

The best, most influential CEOs say, "Pay yourself first, otherwise you will give it all away, and you'll have nothing else left." That is just how the hearts of most people work and they should work this way, because if your heart is filled up you cannot truly give it to anyone else. So give yourself your heart first and then share it with everyone else.

To bring this full circle of how the world is always speaking to you, I remember a woman, who I met eighteen months before I found out I was pregnant, who looked me in the eyes and said, "You are here to do big things; I commend you and honor you. The only advice I can give you is to talk to your soul, grow a relationship with your soul. Talk to your soul just how you would if you desired a new relationship to be birthed." Well, of course, I didn't listen until my life was literally turned upside down, and I had to look at every single part of myself that I hated, had covered up, or had pretended did not exist. The world is always giving you messages through people, so you can remember them at the right moment to get you through any darkness.

I share this with you because what this woman said to me popped into my head shortly after I let go of Ella. Within fifteen minutes of leaving the clinic I pulled over on the side of the road and started writing this book. In that moment, I heard the call of my soul—loud and clear—pulled the heck over, and started typing. I chose to no longer care what the world would think about me from letting my child go; I cared more about expressing my soul's truth so I could heal myself and hopefully help others who have gone through a similar situation. It was in that moment, I overcame the dis-ease of people pleasing because I became *selfishly selfless*, caring more about expressing myself than what other people would think about my truth.

Let's go deeper into being selfishly selfless. What I have learned is that your fridge cannot be filled with things for everyone else when there is nothing in it for you. You should not be driving someone to your house while they ask you, condemningly, if you're on mental medication. You should not be pregnant with someone's child whom you never wanted to be pregnant with. When these things happen, you allowed yourself to be influenced to such a degree that you were more committed to someone else's happiness over your own, which is the dis-ease of pleasing people. Where you are now is not your fault, and to cure the dis-ease of people pleasing you must talk to your soul.

Ask yourself:

➤ My beautiful soul, what makes you happy?

➤ What can I do to hear you more clearly when you are trying to guide and protect me?

➤ What activities can I do to please myself ahead of others?

➤ What judgments about myself can I release?

➤ What new habits can I implement so I feel safe to express myself?

When you ask yourself these simple questions, you are sending a prayer into the universe and you'll start to receive your beautiful soul, so she can guide you out of your pain and suffering and into the life you truly desire to create. You can start to create a life filled with true joy because you became more committed to pleasing yourself, being you, and allowing yourself the gift of expressing who you truly are. Instead of silencing yourself to please others—who will never be as loyal to you as your own soul will be—give voice to your soul. Because remember, when you are busy pleasing others, how can you truly give from an overflowing and abundant cup?

I hope in this chapter you have learned that you have the choice to talk with your soul. Right now is the right time to start pleasing yourself, be loyal to yourself, and stop at nothing to make sure that you treat yourself just as well as you would treat a stranger or even your best friend. You are the most important person in your life, and it's a gift to yourself to start acting that way so you truly can create the changes you desire to see in the world. You can rise up to design, create, and live *An Uncompromised Life* and become the example that shows others what is possible for their lives.

CHAPTER 5

Shifting Generational Lineage

never fully understood generational lineage, honoring our ancestors or even the importance of natives until I got pregnant. I once hired mentors who shared with me that we are impacted by seven generations that come before us. And in turn, we impact seven generations after us. I understood the concept, yet I never actually felt it in my body until I became pregnant. We must understand this on a level that forces us to change our lives. Welcome to lesson number four: shifting generational lineage.

Everything you are up until this point in life is because of what the past seven generations have done for you. At some point in your lineage, there was someone who raised their hand and decided to be a leader—creating a better life for them-selves—or you wouldn't be here reading this book. At some point in your lineage, someone decided they were going to start creating a better social-economic life. This created a ripple effect for you to be here reading this book, because you were passed on the generational lineage to always choose to create a better life than what you had. Or you may be the first in your generational lineage to even have the desire to create a better life, and you will pass that on to the generation below you.

Our Generational Lineage and DNA

I know each of you reading this book has a huge mission, one meant to impact the world, yet you need to be reminded of how important you are in the greater equation of the universe. You may be the first person in your lineage who raised your hand to get a higher education, to choose to read this book on controversial topics, to choose to help others discover a better life through your teachings, life experiences, or a business you will create.

However, there is always a duality to everything. While there have been incredible things in our lineage, there has also been unhealed trauma. Yes, it exists—unresolved trauma of our generational lineage mixed with our past lifetimes can cause us to incur karmic debt. This simply means that we will experience heartache or difficulties, such as an unplanned pregnancy, money issues, a child's death, abuse, a near death experience, or other events. We're meant to use these experiences to heal generational trauma or past lifetime trauma for the generations to come after us and to return to a state of wholeness we didn't know was possible before.

Another way to put it is that we may experience a major life problem through addiction, depression, anxiety, anger, unresolved trauma, lack of emotional intelligence, PTSD, (and the list can go on), yet it's brought to us so we can make it work *for* us—as a greater collective and lineage healing. For example, my paternal grandpa fought in World War II, so there may have been some fierce emotions that he ignored, preventing him from feeling because he had to show up and do what his country required him to do. Well, some of those bottled emotions and his PTSD were passed on to my dad's DNA. My dad ended up having two divorces before he married my mum. Now, they have been married for nearly thirty years. My dad had to go through two divorces to heal from his dad's DNA lineage, which caused a lack of emotional intelligence. Otherwise, he would have avoided getting married to women that weren't for him. However, this was part of his soul contract and karmic debt he agreed to go through this lifetime.

This DNA has been passed down to me, causing my tendencies to be emotionally avoidant and non-committal in love relationships. This is one huge thing I aim to shift in this lifetime. However, do you see how living through World War II (or fighting in any war) would force you to become more emotionally insensitive or lack emotional intelligence? That would be a natural result of anyone forced to go to war by their government. The mind seeks to create stability in the mind and heart through protection mechanisms, which resulted in my grandpa (and many others) not feeling the actions he was doing.

We call this an unconscious coping mechanism, and it exists until we allow ourselves to become aware of it. This coping mechanism becomes what we call coding, which is passed down in our DNA. We must become aware of it within our generational DNA to shift the generational lineage and trauma. Much of the emotional, traumatic events we experience happen so we can become aware of this low-frequency coding and programming that exists in our DNA, and shift it for ourselves and the for the generations ahead of us. That is what it means to start living *An Uncompromised Life*—knowing you aren't just doing things for you, but for the generations to come.

Another example is my maternal grandma had the highest LSAT score in the state of Michigan, yet no law firm would hire her because she was a woman. She was taught to suppress her emotional intelligence because women, for so long, were thought to be unable to work in the marketplace because they were too emotional. This caused her to have awful depression and anxiety later in her life because she had been trained to suppress the truth of who she was. Suppression creates a karmic debt and a malfunction in our body over time. My grandma created a coping mechanism—becoming a workaholic—to avoid her feelings. This worked for her until she no longer worked. Then, this coping mechanism malfunctioned, and she suffered from depression and anxiety at the end of her life. That is why it is so important to start living *An Uncompromised Life* now, because when you make compromises, those moments compound to have a greater impact as you get older. However, my grandma was never aware.

This didn't just stop with my grandma. Her anxiety, depression, people pleasing tendencies, and her intense need to prove her worth as a woman in the workforce was passed onto my beautiful mum. My mum grew up hearing my grandma say, "You always get your guest what they ask for," "You should appear to look a certain way," and "You talk from intelligence." Well, then my mum was gifted a very colorful child from the universe—me—whom she loves so much that she adapted and shifted from more conservative ways of thinking and living to more open, colorful, and imaginative ways so that we could relate at some level. However, it didn't stop at my mum—these DNA traits of anxiety, people pleasing, an extreme need to prove my worth, and passion for woman empowerment were still passed on to me through generational lineage. I believe I am shifting this lineage by no longer working in the matrix of a nine-to-five job. I shifted chronic anxiety by getting myself involved in neurofeedback therapy and I shifted the generational lineage of people pleasing through my choice to let Ella go, forever killing the disease of people pleasing.

In my lineage, I only knew my grandma and mum, yet by understanding what they carried, I can only imagine what the women before them must have carried. No matter what, every generation has created some micro-shift for the better—otherwise, we wouldn't be evolving as a human species.

I realize there is a lot to unpack here.

A question you might be asking is: Do I (or can I) know all of the generational lineage and DNA that has impacted me or is yet to reveal itself? In my opinion, I don't think we can ever know it all, yet it is about becoming a humble student to master ourselves, by becoming curious of traits we resent in our parents, or grandparents and start to become aware how we may carry those same traits within us. Because we cannot see anything in someone else, if it doesn't exist within us.

I am sure in my young twenty-six years, I have only touched the tip of the iceberg on generational lineage and the DNA shifting I am meant to go through. However, this lesson is important for us to learn because this has been deeply encoded into our DNA cells. To complete this idea, bringing it full circle, let me tell you how I know for sure that letting go of Ella was generational lineage being healed.

In the beginning of the book, remember the moment I called my mum, and I shared with her how Ella came to be? Her first response was "Do you know who else's name is Ella?" And I said, "No."

She replied, "Your grandma's best friend's name was Ella, and she was not married and had no children."

When my mum told me this, I experienced chills throughout my entire body because this was the moment when I realized I stopped the generational lineage from being repeated. I cannot make this up! From the little girl telling me her name was Ella when her name was Lila to Ella's dad giving me the toy unicorn he had named El and discovering my grandma's best friend was named Ella, there were three confirmations—a trinity: mind, body, and soul, a divine confirmation this whole experience was bigger than just me.

Parenting Consequences

Finally, I understood not just the *theory* of shifting generational lineage, but I *felt* it. My mum's and dad's individual purposes in life revolved around having a family and children—before they even meet each other. I truly believe the reason they got married is because they both loved each other, but they both wanted to have a family and be good parents, too. This purpose is what allowed them to stay in love for thirty-plus years. My parents, their parents, and seven generations before me—their lives circled around their kids and families. I can tell you my mum changed career paths from lawyer to school teacher, just so she could substitute teach in my classes, be home more, and spend more time with me. Then, she went back to working as a lawyer once I went to college. There is nothing wrong with this. It shows how she wanted to be a great mother and be with me because she loved me that much, which I will be forever grateful for. Neither of my parents really allowed themselves to have an energy source outside of me. I was what gave them life, instead of them already feeling whole, complete, and happy with or without me there. Some people might argue this is a very beautiful parenting model.

However, this creates an issue. My parents needed me. I'd argue they needed me just as much as they needed oxygen—especially my mum. This "needing" of another created a codependent loop, especially traumatic within the mother-daughter bond. Many of us have subconscious codependent loops with objects, some with other people, and some are attached to receiving results. This codependency has been passed on from generation to generation, especially in the context of children. When—as parents—we allow ourselves to become dependent on sourcing our purpose through our children, we mistakenly believe once we become a parent or have a family, we will feel whole. Which means we are missing the point of feeling whole and complete *now*, creating an unhealthy relationship. The child grows up feeling like they must always be the source of happiness for their parents. This belief system could lead to the child accepting narcissistic relationships or emotionally unavailable people, because that child has learned to be the sole provider of their parents' happiness—depleting their energy to always pleasing other people first.

Of course, all of this occurs on a completely unconscious level—we are unaware. My parents are both incredible people, parents that would never have intended to do this. They love me and do so much for me, they were just never taught how to be complete on their own without needing to take those things from their relationship with their child. They simply learned this from their parents and so on, so it is a generational loop.

I cannot be angry at them, but I can educate them (and you) through this book. Because being unaware is the very reason I became pregnant . . . and now I've become aware of this. I've shifted it from my generational lineage by letting Ella go, so it won't repeat the same pattern. Again, I would have been having Ella to appease her dad and his desires, rather than what was best for my life journey, which was not to have a child at that time. Then from this I took action to educate the collective whole on this topic of generational lineage as I experienced it.

Do you see how big and miraculous this life can be for you, once you realize that none of the perceived traumatic things that happen to you actually happened *to* you? They happened *for* you—for your highest growth and evolution. Trauma happens in order for us to learn, grow, and evolve—and then share it with the collective so others can grow through our story. One of the big-picture reasons I got pregnant was to heal the generational DNA and lineage of people pleasing, increase my emotional intelligence, and end codependent looping. I'm sure there are more reasons I will still discover as they are revealed to me in time. Yet, my commitment to transmute my pain of letting Ella go is what compelled me to write this book—revealing to me why Ella even happened. In writing this book I created my own healing journey and I know it is meant to help countless women and men that read this book in so many ways.

I want to share something I wrote in April of 2019 on Facebook, as it relates to not needing to always know why things are happening in our life, yet learning to trust there is a greater purpose for it. In this post I talk about codependency. If you are living your life for your kids, your work, or your life partner, this post applies to you. Co-dependency can manifest in forms of addiction, low self-esteem, weight issues, trauma, and the list can go on. My spiritual co-dependency manifested in having an unplanned pregnancy. I never knew why I wrote this post, yet when I was writing this book, I realized it was for this book . . . Generational lineage works this way, we don't need to know why we got the mom, dad, grandparents, or great grandparents we did; we just need to trust that there's a greater reason for why we were birthed into a certain family lineage. We must trust there are certain traits that we received and know we have the opportunity to completely shift the traits in our lineage.

I hope you relate to these words, as I wrote them seven months before I became pregnant, which goes to show that I understood codependency and people pleasing at a theoretical level, yet I was not able to completely feel, heal, and embody it at a DNA level.

Codependency

I feel the pendulum swinging, time and time again.

My emotions get high and then low.

I feel certain in who I am and then I feel completely lost at the same time.

To avoid feeling anything less than perfect, I obsessively point my focus at a target or goal (whatever that may be), and I stop at nothing until I get to that destination.

Then once I reach the destination, I decide it is not good enough, so I start to obsess over something bigger, something larger to again avoid looking at the beautiful journey I was able to live—to the destination I just obsessed over.

This pattern has gone on my whole life, and I keep praying to Source that I PROMISE this is the last goal, the last destination I will obsess over, I promise THEN I will feel complete in my harmonization journey.

Not realizing that this the same pattern I do time and time again, to realize that unity with harmonization is a JOURNEY.

Each time I create movement it only expands the existing circle I am in, shape shifting me into another reality I could have never imagined, because it's better than what the mind could ever comprehend to create.

I keep putting all the desires, all the movement, all the momentum on that SHINY object right above where I can currently reach, to then always obsessively achieve it, yet missing the journey of being present in my body while I went through the whole experience.

I create this codependent relationship with friendships, social media, the need to be admired, my phone, objects, achieving goals and isolating myself in order to play around and research my addiction to love.

I create this codependent ideology that love can only exist when I hear the three words "I LOVE YOU" instead of being present with actions, lessons, and experiences.

As I share this, I am not sure if you can relate, however I am here to remind you that love starts from within always and forever . . . NO matter how much you desire, you try, you obsess over creating the magical lifestyle of love around you, it's remembering that it already exists within you RIGHT NOW.

Within this beautiful post, I already knew (at the theoretical level) to get away from Ella's dad, because he was not good for me. I knew he wasn't good for me because from an early stage, he used to tell me, "I love you," which is exactly what my codependent coding needed to hear to keep me stuck in old patterns. We all know what our patterns are, yet we avoid looking at them, because we think they will simply go away.

My parents lived their lives for me, which means I got used to being a source for other people's love and energy instead of using my own energy to love myself. I never learned what true love meant. I created the same scenario where I would be the source of love for someone else, even if they were unable to meet my needs because I was taught as a child to always source other people first. This is a perfect example of how generational lineage and DNA plays out.

Through this beautiful unplanned pregnancy, after medical doctors told me I would need to change my medication to become pregnant, I was guided to make the empowered decision to source myself *for myself*, instead of allowing my body to be used for someone else's intentions, which were not aligned with mine. I truly believe that even if I had taken birth control measures, this same story would've unfolded because it was a soul contract of mine for my soul's highest growth and to be used for a collective healing. It was meant as a way to explain the unexplainable and remind us just how powerful our experiences are. And our experiences should be shared. Our traumas did not happen *to* us, they happened *for* us so we can release the judgment and shame around them because we are completing a soul contract or karmic debt with our life experiences.

In conclusion, what I wish I would've known and am now imprinting to you is: Never make any of this life—the good or the bad—about you. In every moment, there is soul expansion available for you. You can experience more joy because you freaking deserve it. And once you're happy, other people will see your joy, and instead of stealing it from you, they'll learn how to activate their own inner joy. Your joy is coming from a different place now. You are no longer carrying generational lineage that is teaching you to give everything away, suppress your feelings, or strive to be successful at the cost of your own happiness. You may have trauma occur for you to realize this codependent looping, addiction coding, suffering programming, false money stories, self-worth issues, and more. However, this trauma happens so all of this can come to your awareness, to heal the issues in your generational lineage (that were present far before you were ever conceived in someone's beautiful womb). This trauma occurred for your future to be more expansive and for your children, your grandchildren, and even your friends' children to be impacted by you in such a way that they start to see they are safe to be themselves in your presence.

The root of all this stems from people, who at some point in their lives, felt they had to stop expressing a part of themselves in order to feel safe and achieve a desired result. It stems from the values and moral system that was placed on them. This is why Ella was such a gift—I can now easily discern and be aware of when I am going through a generational lineage shift for a greater collective awareness and to impact the seven generations to come after me in my lineage.

The key to living *An Uncompromised Life* is for you to start embodying new layers of the true expression of you by letting go of generational lineage and DNA that no longer serves you. You can guide yourself to drop your own walls, feel safe to express yourself always, instead of compromising your truest expression to please others. This is the moment when generational lineage is shifted and miracles are birthed because you realize none of your hardships are actually about you; they are for something much greater—for generations down the line that we will never know. Whatever personal or traumatic experience happened, it occurred through you to teach you to honor yourself over anyone else, so you can shift the generational lineage you received, passing on better DNA coding to your future lineage.

CHAPTER 6

Letting Go

L etting go—lesson five—has been the most challenging lesson for me to integrate in my life. Both the idea and action of letting go keep coming back to me in various ways. Most of our lessons continue to come through in different situations and people as we come into more expansive states in life (since the universe is always testing us to see if we are truly committed to our evolution).

The more we begin to open our eyes and allow ourselves to see just how important we are within the greater equation of the universe, new things will be demanded of us. In order for us to become who we are meant to be, there are more things we have to become aware of and let go of. Everything we have ever known has gotten us to this point, yet for where we are going, we have to let go of everything we have ever known to make room for new ideas, changes, lessons, and lifestyles that are available to us.

Let's talk about when I started to let go of Ella's dad *energetically*. The day I told him about my miscarriage, he said that he needed space and didn't talk to me for five days. However, when he needed my help to write his first book and do sales funnels, he flew back to Los Angeles the next day.

This is when my head started to spiral with things that were not making sense in our relationship. From the outside looking in, the writing had been written in black and white letters: He did not care about making time to be there with me through my emotions from a miscarriage, yet he did make the time to capitalize on my talents—for his gain—for his book and funnels. However, it's not his fault nor is he to blame, because it was in my unawareness that I allowed him in and co-created this darkness. It was in that moment, I made the decision I was going to take action and start letting go of him, admitting to myself it was an abortion instead of a miscarriage, and letting go of the trauma an abortion brings.

Then all of a sudden, Melanie Tonia Evans came across my computer, and I signed up for her sixteen-day newsletter on how to overcome narcissistic abuse. This is what started building my courage to stop all communication with Ella's dad—I felt a lot of judgment, shame, and guilt come up that I needed to let go of. How did a smart woman like me fall for someone like this? Everything was obvious in hindsight—clear as day—and when I removed myself from the relationship, I wondered why I had not been able to see it while I was in the thick of it.

Melanie helped me realize some things. Ella's dad wanted children. His one partner I knew didn't want kids. On top of this they tried to get me to put my life savings into their company. Given this information, it wasn't hard for me to believe they had crafted a plan for me, unknown to me. They had tried to convince me to invest my money in their company before I got pregnant. And don't forget about that random card from the woman who was Facebook friends with Ella's dad and from the same city and state Ella's dad grew up in, providing a congratulatory message about me having a baby before I was even pregnant.

There's too much evidence here for me not to believe this was pre-planned by the universe, co-created by all of us, and made into reality to teach me a lesson. Luckily, I trusted my gut, and I said no to a baby and no to giving them my money.

However, my subconscious was forcing me to stay stuck in an addictive looping pattern, trying to figure out how this all happened instead of just letting it go. This happens when we focus on others and avoid looking within. It's like when we don't show up for fitness class, yet we always feel tired and fat and talk to everyone we know about how good everyone else looks. The very thing that would fix the whole problem is to stop talking about it and start showing up at the gym. However, our subconscious mind is convincing us to avoid showing up to the gym because it wants us to stay in the habit of knowing how to suffer—that is more familiar than the unknown. Well, I refused to suffer forever. I asked God for a sign—anything to get me out of this addictive mindset, which was looping awful thoughts about myself.

Shortly after I started asking for help, I stopped focusing on how stupid I was and started asking the universe how people could do this to someone's life. Through the grace of God, when I became emotionally available for support, Melanie sent out an email that she had a live training she was going to offer. I signed up for it immediately; however, it was eight days away. I literally thought I might go crazy while waiting the eight days to listen to what this woman would have to say about how to let go of the past. I felt like a drug addict needing relief from a drug I didn't even know existed (which is exactly how narcissism works).

I knew I had to take action and do something so I could start to let go before the eighth day arrived. I wanted to move through the trauma of letting Ella go, the shame for lying about the abortion, and the judgment of ending up in such a crazy relationship. So, I went to Melanie's YouTube channel and binge-watched her videos—all in one night. Nothing changed. I still felt like a drug addict needing relief.

I thought to myself, "Okay, forget this. Maybe her webinar cannot help me, and I am just totally doomed."

A couple of nights later, I was up late and thought I'd give this woman another listen, with a different energy. Instead of me being frantic, like a drug addict seeking a quick fix, I decided to go with the mindset of listening to her with the energy that says "I'm open to receive and be healed."

Four hours into listening to Melanie Tonia Evans on YouTube (which by the way is *completely free*), I was able to let it *all* go. I didn't just let the relationship go. I let every previous heartbreak go; I let go of every trauma with my parents; I let go of lying about the abortion; I let go of the trauma I had with money. I literally understood how to let anything go—regardless of what it was.

What was the difference between the one night of being frustrated, stuck, and feeling totally doomed versus the night I was able to let it all go? The first night, I showed up to the videos *needing* help, thinking there was something wrong with me. I thought that with someone else helping me, I would get through the pain and push through to the other side.

This is a powerful avoidant and codependent tactic that we use because we have not learned to trust ourselves. We have given our power away and convinced ourselves to trust other people more than we trust ourselves. I had been doing this throughout my whole life, because from a young age my parents programmed me to trust them more than I trusted myself. If others say (even with the best of intentions), "We know what is best for you," it's false. No one knows what is best for you except you. If our parents haven't done their own inner work, they won't know it's actually in the best interest of their children to speak up and share what they believe is best for them.

We have been trained to seek confirmation from others for doing the "right" thing. Students think they need an A+ to know they are doing a good job. In reality, if science is not part of our divine mission, and we are being forced to learn it, then a C+ is great. If we are average in science (and that's okay), we can focus our extra energy on doing our best in math, because perhaps that is more aligned with our purpose. We must let go of the illusion that everyone needs an A+ in every subject, because it causes a lot of disruption in our internal guidance system—when we force ourselves to do something that does not excite us. We are trying to push ourselves to be wizards in something not meant for our souls' true calling in this life.

Only you know what is best for you, so always focus on *you*—not other people, their opinions, or what they have done. I knew leaving the relationship with Ella's dad was what was best for me a long before I became pregnant. Yet I couldn't let it go because I wouldn't accept the lesson that I needed to change—to love and honor myself—but instead I kept going into the fire of allowing a reality I didn't want to live in.

When you admit to knowing what is best for you and let go of everything else, you just outsmarted the system. Most parents, schools, and leaders are not aware of this inner guidance system we have, of always knowing what is best for ourselves. Instead, people try to convince us that what is best for them is what is best for us, which is simply not true. This is how Ella's dad hooked me in—because I wanted to understand the game of money, and I thought he knew money. The reality is: I already knew the game of money and how it should work for me. I just wasn't ready to let go of the false illusion that there is only one way to success.

The night everything shifted for me with Melanie Tonia Evans' videos, I realized I was trying to work all this out in my head. I was trying to lecture myself out of the situation, and I was trying to logically justify (to myself) that I was not stupid.

I just couldn't understand how on earth this situation could happen to me. I. learned quickly trying to talk our way out of something simply doesn't work. We cannot call people and ask them how they overcame the death of a child, a divorce, or their heartbreak and expect it to help us. It just does not work because we are attempting to avoid feeling the pain in our own bodies—trying to solve a problem logically—when the problem is not logical.

Melanie taught me that we must drop into our bodies, feel where the pain is, and then simply request for it to leave. Ask light to come in to fill the new empty space.

I did this, and was immediately able to let go of so many toxic and traumatic experiences held in my body. I literally sat straight up in my chair. I took a deep breath. I closed my eyes, and rolled my eyes toward my third eye (the space between your two eyes). I felt the pain in my womb (sacral chakra) and core (solar plexus chakra). And I said, "God, please release this pain. I no longer allow this coding and imprinting within my body. I no longer accept this within my cellular coding."

AND OH BOY, I WAS IN FOR A SURPRISE.

I released five to eight huge breaths that felt like huge yawns escaping my mouth. I felt ten energy contractions release from my vaginal area. Then, I just sat there with tears streaming down my face. "I DID IT!"

I had released the cellular memory of the trauma of letting go of a child that had been toxically encoded in my DNA. It was in that moment, I started screaming, "Thank you, thank you, thank you!"

I was home alone in my apartment. It was 2:00 a.m. My pink rose quartz crystal started to flicker again.

"Oh my gosh! Ella, you are here with me! WE DID IT!"

From that moment, my life would never be the same because I saw how easy this process of letting go was. Pain is inevitable, yet forcing ourselves to suffer is optional. It does not have to take a lifetime, or even a lot of time, to overcome heartbreak or trauma. It can happen instantly when we choose to drop from our heads and into our bodies. We can feel where the trauma has been toxically implanted in our body. We can simply choose to let it go and let the unexplainable miracles of the universe take care of the rest.

Otherwise, all we're doing when we allow ourselves to stay stuck in the same pattern over and over again is create an addiction to suffering. This is not your fault because the trauma is stored in your body, which is in your DNA at a cellular level (Chapter 5 reference). Many of us are unaware of this or subconsciously avoid this because our brains are trained to keep us doing the same habits, we've always done.

The process I just outlined for you doesn't even take two minutes. However, it's not just about the process; it's about how you show up to the process. Are you showing up to the process as I initially did—*needing* a quick fix? If so, you are actually bypassing the ability to feel the beauty of the release. Or are you showing up with curiosity and a true desire to receive healing from the universe?

It's a lot like sex. Would you want to just show up to have the quick release of an organism, or do you want to take your time and truly feel every sensation and contraction move through your body, begging to be released? All of us, I am sure, would choose to slow it down and feel the beauty of every sensation move through us.

It is a simple yet powerful shift that needs to occur for you to instantly let go of whatever is holding you back. The shift will free you for the rest of your life. However, even though I let go of the trauma from releasing a child, I still placed so much judgement on myself for allowing this situation to happen in my life. After fully letting go of the trauma in my body, I came to realize we still must learn to forgive ourselves for the judgment we've placed on ourselves. Forgiveness occurs when we allow ourselves to be fully grateful for whatever traumatic event or perceived injustice has happened to us.

For example, when I went $100,000 in debt, I remember having no emotions about it. I thought, "It just is what it is. I know that I will come out of this."

My dad was the one who loaned me the money so that I could pay the banks back. Except, I still hadn't learned my lesson—I went right back into debt!

Most of you may be thinking, "What the heck? How and why on earth would you do that?" When I look at where most of my money went, it was into personal development, retreats, online programs, coaches, therapists, holistic healers, yoga, and food. It did not matter what I was spending the money on, because I was spending it to avoid looking within. The core reason for me spending insane amounts of money was because I did not yet understand how to let go of the traumatic coding that was imprinted in my cellular DNA. I couldn't release the judgement that I felt; this was the worst thing ever. I tried to fix my problem of getting into debt, but I still continued to judge myself for falling into the trap with money again.

I engaged in negative self-talk, the same way I used negative self-talk about becoming pregnant.

Why did I trust the doctors?

Why wasn't I smarter?

Why didn't I get out of the unhealthy relationship?

This is me getting lost in my mind, going in circles, trying to logically talk my way out of something that is not logical. Can you relate?

Whenever we have major trauma, health issues, money issues, or relationship issues, it is a defect caused by us not listening to our emotions or paying attention to signs the universe is giving us to move in a different direction. The universe wants every single person to feel happy, fulfilled, and good. If, after some time, you choose to remain stuck—a creature to your habits of suffering—that is when a major malfunction happens to our energetic system and an explosive situation unfolds in our lives.

For me, going back into debt was because I didn't address the real problem. The foundational issue was that I didn't understand what it meant to accept myself and every part of my journey that has shaped me. I realized that my heart was hurting because I had tied my self-worth to the amount of money I was making, instead of feeling whole and complete regardless of the dollar amount that was in my bank account.

I still carried shame and guilt about not figuring out how to manage my money, instead of going into a state of gratitude. Thankfully I was able to learn this lesson at age twenty-six, before I started managing bigger amounts of money in my life.

I could not get myself out of the loop of feeling sorry for myself which kept me from moving into an empowered state. So, I repeated these mantras—these truths—to myself:

➤ I accept myself for making the same decision twice.

➤ I accept that I was just spending to avoid looking at my real problems.

➤ I accept the fact that I said yes and let people steal my money because there was a learning lesson in it for me.

➤ I accept that I was freely giving my money away while expecting so little in return.

From this place of acceptance, the process of letting go becomes much faster and easier. I learned I needed to start putting myself first, before everyone else. The same problem of not putting myself first had produced three different defects: having an unplanned pregnancy, going into debt twice, and having more in my fridge for others than I did for myself. It took all three of these experiences for me to come back to the same conclusion: *I must love myself.* When you come to this awareness, the only outcome is to become grateful. I had learned to make sense of the insensible. What a gift that I learned these hard lessons at age twenty-six instead of fifty-five.

How magnificent is this world that all these perceived problems arose in my life so I could understand that I am such an extraordinary and miraculous human? I realized I was giving all of myself to everyone . . . except me. I had to change that narrative, and this may be the very lesson you need to learn from this book as well.

God used my circumstances and relationships to show me that when I compromise my body, my character, and my values by not loving and honoring myself, all of these problems would continue to occur in my life. Instead, I needed to move into living *An Uncompromised Life*. We do not have to live a lifetime full of guilt and shame. In an instant we can transmute our stories and traumas for a higher purpose and interweave it into a business mission to serve others.

I promise, the moment you start to do this—let go of whatever it is you so badly want to overcome—everything shifts in an instant. You no longer have to live stuck in a story where the healing never comes. The reality is that right now you are alive, you are breathing, and you have the opportunity to create miracle after miracle in your life and in the lives of others.

If you choose to avoid your problems by doing more, achieving more, and winning more, you are missing the point and won't find that freedom you so badly desire. You'll continue seeking out things that won't fulfill your soul's purpose:

➤ Money
➤ Relationship
➤ New Clothes
➤ A House
➤ To be a Parent

That thing your soul desires will not show up until you get present, let go of the cellular trauma in your body, and become grateful for whatever the heck you think you can avoid and cover up, making it look nice and pretty to the world.

Acknowledge that you co-created all the perceived "negative" things that have happened. Those experiences needed to happen to evolve your soul into who you are meant to become. Love every person and everything that made the experience possible. Without them, you would not have learned, evolved, and grown. You wouldn't have been able to understand the process of letting go. Now you get to feel and experience life on a deeper and more meaningful level.

From this new place, you'll realize the greatest lessons will come and come again. Wherever you are heading in your beautiful life requires more of your subconscious to be brought into awareness, so you can feel it, heal it, and let go of it so it comes out on the other side.

In this practice of letting go, you'll find forgiveness, pure gratitude, and acceptance that lessons will always show up in your life—you cannot avoid them. Embrace them, choose to see the silver lining, and understand there is a beautiful message for you in the storm. That thing you so badly want to achieve right now cannot be manifested into your reality without you letting go of something you are subconsciously holding onto.

Letting go is a process of teaching you to be present in the now, instead of trying to rush through something to get to a desired result in the future. That is how so many of us do life, and that is why so many people die without living a fulfilled life. That is why the world creates these atomic bombs that go off in our lives . . . so we can slow down and ask ourselves, "What do I need to become aware of and let go of, so I can actually be happy, healthy, and whole?"

It is only in being present, in the now, that your greatest power comes. This is where your creativity is birthed. This is where you become free and escape the slavery of mind programming, which was never yours to carry. Now is when you forgive everyone who has brought you anger, because you see they are simply a reflection of your shadow self you are choosing to ignore.

That is when you will see the beautiful power of how easy it is to let go of others, because they are just a reflection of you. When you initiate yourself into a new layer of who you are, it becomes easy to let go of things you no longer wish to experience, empowering you to be grateful because you start to see the results that you are growing. You'll find a newfound love and appreciation for yourself and humanity, instead of searching for love from humanity to fill in the gaps where you lacked giving love to yourself.

This is the power within the journey of letting go. It allows old parts of you (that are not meant to come with you) to die while empowering new parts of you to be birthed.

Anything you desire and more is already waiting for you to grab it.

➤ Look within and ask where the trauma is existing in your body.
➤ Create your own mantra to release it.
➤ Allow the unexplainable universe to take care of the rest.

➤ Finally, allow yourself to fall in love with the process of letting go over and over again in this beautiful life, so the true purity of who you really are can shine through.

CHAPTER 7

Owning Your No to Live a Heck Yes Life

et's address something directly—the question of how I got pregnant when medical doctors told me I would need to switch my thyroid medication in order to have the correct hormone levels to ever become pregnant. At the time of writing this book, I haven't been on thyroid medication for over three years. I haven't been to a doctor checkup appointment in nearly four years.

These same doctors initially told me I would need to be on medication for the rest of my life, and I have been off the medication since I started following my dreams in March of 2017. From that moment forward, I learned that what medical doctors say means nothing compared to your intentions and the miracles that occur when we align with the universe.

Well, let's dive into this next lesson, number six. There are two specific reasons I believe I became pregnant, despite not taking medication or changing the dosage of any medication.

The first reason is the power of two. When people are in union together as friends, business partners, lovers, or any other close relationship, the power of two births a third entity. When one or two people together have thoughts, intentions, or are making constant jokes about something happening, that "something" usually happens quicker than we think it should. However, this is not the lesson, or reason, I want to focus on in this particular book.

The second reason is because I was saying yes to so many things when I really wanted to say no. I was betraying my body by drinking, partying, and having sex when I didn't necessarily want to do those things. I was putting on a face that told others I was okay with doing something, when in my heart, my body was repulsed by it all. Often, I would go out and drink to numb my feelings about everything I was doing.

It was a lot like if you are forcing yourself to go to school, work a job, or hang out with people just because you think that is what you are supposed to do. Yet you are suffering from depression, anxiety, PTSD, addiction, avoidance behavior, attachment issues, workaholism, or eating disorders. The actual health disorder or physically manifested problem is never the real root issue of these physical or mental health issues. The unplanned pregnancy, anxiety, depression, PTSD, avoidance behavior, etc. are more like malfunctions from you doing things you truly don't want to do. Overtime these malfunctions compound into a greater problem that you eventually cannot ignore.

From the outside, it seemed I had created my dream life; but I was saying yes to the wrong relationships. I created the wrong relationships the minute I got into business because I wanted to learn from people who would teach me how to make money, instead of learning from people who would genuinely help me learn how to master myself and share my gifts to help others. This resulted in me co-creating many relationships (including the one with Ella's dad) where I thought they would teach me something about money or business that I didn't know, but that never happened. I genuinely cared about these mentors and people in my life. Yet, I also thought I needed them to help my mission, which stems from the codependent wounding I talked about in Chapter 5.

This codependency resulted in me saying yes to things I did not want to really do, because I wanted them to like me and think I was worthy of their time to help me. This stems from a false sense of validation. All of this ended in the ultimate atomic bomb going off in my life—becoming pregnant. Becoming pregnant was not just from me saying yes to doing things or going places with Ella's dad when I meant no. It was from *all* the times, compounded over many years, of saying yes when I wanted to say no in relationships. This was compounded from every person I thought I needed to please so they might help me with my business and impact goals. All the days I stayed in corporate when I should have left, and all the money I lent to friends when I really didn't want to do that.

We do not keep track of our mindless actions, but our hearts do. When we say yes when we really mean no, these experiences compound over time. Much like finances compound overtime, when you emotionally abuse yourself, your mind may not be keeping score, but your heart and body are. This place of saying yes to things when you mean no compounds overtime and creates a catastrophic event like cancer, a death, a major illness or an unplanned pregnancy. You cannot judge yourself for saying yes when you meant no, because this is a *powerful* lesson that we chose to go through before incarnating as a human. We chose our parents, our friends, our schools, our children (if we have them), our lovers—everything—because we are meant to learn powerful lessons from them, to complete our soul contracts, and assist in other people's evolutions through our life experiences.

I didn't become pregnant just because I always said yes to Ella's dad. It was throughout my whole life that I betrayed my body with men, drinking, and drugs because I was never taught how to say no. It's none of these men's fault because I probably appeared present in the moment; yet in reality, I was totally disconnected from my body and many times, I would actually leave my body, so I didn't have to be aware of what was going on. Within this story, I subconsciously agreed to be in a relationship dynamic that was emotionally killing me behind closed doors.

I figured if I just kept showing up that somehow it would all get better or change.

That is a lie—programming I learned from my mum and grandma—to just keep showing up, regardless of how miserable it is because that is what you are meant to do to prove your place in the world as a woman.

Why did this happen? So, I would learn the lesson of what happens when you continuously betray yourself. For me, this was having an unplanned pregnancy I never knew was possible, that I then chose to let go of.

Yet, I chose to go through this before I came here in human form, as God needed this "blessing in disguise" to come through me for this book to be written. It's the same reason I was diagnosed with cancer at such a young age, so people could learn their health issues usually stem from emotional suppression and not expressing who you truly are meant to be.

Both cancer and my pregnancy happened in order for me to understand the power within me—creating my reality. Up until this point, I allowed myself to live a somewhat false life. We all do this at times, because we are meant to be evolving. We always have the opportunity to evolve, yet sometimes we consciously or subconsciously choose to stay stuck. Whatever the reason is for us choosing to stay stuck is where the miracles and lessons are birthed.

When we say yes when we mean no in an effort to avoid hurting someone else's feelings, a small lie is born. Over time, these small lies compound into a huge, catastrophic event. Many times, when we are saying yes when we mean no, we don't even realize it is a form of lying or being fake. We think we are doing everyone else a favor. Again, this is a frequency that was passed down to us; we have been taught to be fake and lie by Disney movies and Hollywood to receive love, to say yes to our bosses so we get the raise, and to say things we don't mean because we think we have to in order to get what we want. We cannot be critical of ourselves for doing this. We must learn to accept the fact that we have an opportunity to evolve through it. Because our HECK YES life is still to come as we practice our honest no.

My first honest no was in choosing to let go of Ella. I didn't call Ella's dad to talk about it, and I didn't even admit what I chose to do to myself for quite some time. I called it a voluntary miscarriage because I was not ready to understand everything that had happened. As time passed, I understood that letting go of Ella was the birth of my new life and of many more new lives that I will continue to birth within this lifetime. I know if I had called Ella's dad and told him the truth, my reality would be very different right now. I don't know if I would have been strong enough to stand my ground and say no, doing what was best for me. It was already so painful; I didn't need anyone else influencing me at the time. What allowed me to be strong is that I truly heard God talking to me, telling me to not call Ella's dad.

Through this whole process, I listened to God for when to sit in stillness, when to phone friends, and when to tell my parents, which was quite a while afterwards. This was my beautiful journey of owning my no, which birthed an epic learning process where I would no longer feel compelled and called to share every detail of my life with every person until I felt ready to do so. That is exactly how God wanted me to evolve through this, to share this beautiful story.

The only reason I was able to follow through on my choice with Ella is because I heard the voices of God and the universe speaking to me. I have learned, though, you cannot hear the voice of God, the universe, angels, or whatever else you want to call it, if you are blindly showing up for everyone else, worried about what they're thinking, and your more afraid of disappointing them than being true to yourself. I knew if I decided to call Ella's dad, the voice of the universe would be silenced through me. Deep down, I wanted to please him, because I thought he was going to help me in ways I couldn't help myself. Yet something deep inside of me knew I had to be more committed to the universe speaking to me in this moment, than I was committed to pleasing someone else.

It was in this moment that I knew this was something I had to go through alone—to be in silence so I could hear the universe's voice coming through me. This is something many of us need to train ourselves to do—sit in the quiet. Otherwise, we can't hear our honest noes and yesses. Instead we get so far into our environments, where people influence us to easily say yes; we feel trapped, in chaos so deep we cannot pull out. We may have structured our financial life around something, we may have kids with someone, our healthcare may be tied to a job, we may share a business with a partner . . . whatever it is, we are in so deep that our life is co-created with something or someone in such a way that we cannot hear our honest no screaming for us to get out of a situation that is hijacking us.

For example, when I was in corporate America, I hated it. No way would I stay up working until 2:00 or 3:00 a.m. The only reason I worked was to make money. This was a false life I was living, because I was saying yes to something I hated, simply to earn money. That money was never actually going to let me live the life I wanted because I was suffering while working, so I couldn't be creating the HECK YES life experiences that I deeply desired. In Chapter 3, we discussed it's simply a universal law: You cannot be doing something you hate and expect to create a lifestyle you love without changing any of your actions. I stayed in corporate longer than I wanted to because I didn't know how I was going to get healthcare with pre-existing conditions. I thought I was trapped instead of owning my no and getting the heck out. You may be mindlessly going through ignoring your no, but your body and your heart are keeping score. Eventually, saying yes to things you really want to say no to will manifest into a big, traumatic experience in your life that you cannot ignore; over time you allowed yourself to not be honest with what you were feeling and what you were doing in your life.

So what are the steps you can take to get more comfortable with saying no?

I believe, ultimately, it's when you start to believe you have a higher purpose or calling that you take the first step. From that place of knowing you have a higher purpose, your life shifts rapidly. I have seen this with thousands of people I have helped since the age of fourteen. Once you realize that it is your duty to figure out why you are here on this earth, it is easy to say no to anything or anyone that would distract you from that calling. And your calling is always evolving.

When I first left my corporate job, I thought I was meant to spread love and travel the world. Now, I know I am meant to bridge business, spirituality, entrepreneurship, and academia. I had to go through larger and more catastrophic experiences and lessons for me to learn the next layer of my calling. Yet I am grateful for them because without going through the hard times, I couldn't be prepared for what is still to come.

A business-minded example of this phenomenon is when we say yes to every single idea that flows through us. If you're like me, you have a million voices going on in your head, and you have a million ideas flowing through your brain. You believe you can help anyone start a business or you can help everyone fix any problem. Well, you haven't met the one idea—the one thing—that is going to set you free, so you stop saying yes to everything, instead you start to own your no. When you're living a compromised life you are "going with the flow," in no real direction.

The art of living *An Uncompromised Life* is when you finally feel free to be you, you say no to the things you don't want to do, and you start allowing yourself to feel liberated in the things you do desire. When you live a life of compromised moments you may have said yes to hanging out with friends you didn't really want to be with, you may have said yes to going to that event with someone because it was better than being at home alone and reading. Let me tell you . . . from traveling all over the world, moving five different times to four different states in America in under five years, say no to the people and things that do not excite you. Regardless of how badly you want to spend time with people, how obsessed you are with "looking cool," how afraid you are to stay at home alone with yourself, stop doing things you truly don't want to do. Your soul, your heart, and your being want you to be happy. When you are spending time, energy, and focus on doing everything and not slowing down to assess yourself and how you're feeling in the process, you're missing the whole point of living life. You are numbing yourself, being fake, and having no real interest in being true to you. You'll end up not having a clue what to talk about when you're in these environments because *the real you doesn't even want to be there.*

Here is the key: We all have these experiences. We all have said yes when we meant no. It's *letting go* of judgment and shame and simply allowing yourself to become aware of these experiences so you start saying no to distractions and finding your calling. I used to think I needed a relationship to be successful. After this experience, I would always say no to any and all relationships that did not meet my basic needs. I would say no to business partnerships that did not feel equal. However, the biggest way for you to own your no is to slow down and ask yourself, "How is my life the way it is? How can my life's hardships be served for a greater purpose?" Then you'll realize more hardships will arise that you are simply meant to learn from, so you can help more people by living into the next layer of your life's calling.

From this, learn to be okay with silence—so you can hear the messages of the universe or in the stillness, you can actually start to feel what is present for you on your heart. Every time you ignore the messages from the universe or you refuse to communicate what is truly on your heart, your body creates a chemical reaction. Over time, this chemical reaction can create things like cancer, viruses, unwanted pregnancies, and more. A great book to read further about this is *The Emotion Code* by Dr. Bradley Nelson, or there is one by Louise Hays called *Heal Your Body.*

By denying communication of what is really on your heart and mind, you're hindering someone else's evolution as well. Many times, we create this story that no one is going to understand us, so if we say no it's going to cause a disagreement— we decide it's "just" better to keep the peace. When something is on your heart, it's there because a certain frequency and transmission is coming through you. Think about it. Everything around us, including ourselves, can be measured back to a Hz frequency—this is science. The words we use each have a different frequency. An example of this is when music artists sing the same song over and over and over again until they get their desired pitch, which is simply a frequency measured in Hz vibration from soundboards. When you stop yourself from speaking words that are on your heart and mind, you are blocking the natural movement of a sound vibration that should move through you and out into the world. This, as I mentioned before, then creates suppressed emotions which can lead to a toxic chemical reaction in the body.

Another way to think about this is: We each have a lot of energy and emotions that are always on our hearts and minds, which we desire to share—this is the truest expression of us.

So start to think of your truest expression like a train going full force; the truest expression of you wants to be able to move through you. It wants to be let out into the world. Yet every time you deny yourself the opportunity to share what is really on your heart and mind, it's like that train, going full force within you, is forced to slam on the brakes. Well, that doesn't end well for anyone—the passengers, the train's wheels, or the tracks. The train created an alarming experience by halting on the brakes because for whatever reason, it just decided it no longer wanted to travel down the path it was going. When you don't communicate what is on your heart and mind in each moment, you are basically slamming on the breaks of a train within your own body because you're denying yourself your right to express *you*. A lifetime of doing this to yourself will absolutely have a taxing effect on your body and emotions, just as it would damage a train car, a regular car, or anything else.

A real-life example of this is: Two people are going to an event because they think that is what the other person wants to do, when in reality, neither of them want to go. They'd rather hang out at home. Now, both people are showing up from a perceived "false" illusion of pleasing the other, and neither person wants to be at the event. Neither person spoke up to own his or her no. So now these two people are both at an event they don't want to be at, instead of possibly creating a heck yes moment for them if they had been honest with each other and both admitted they wanted to stay home.

What I have learned from my unplanned pregnancy and life experiences is that the more we can become aware of the events in our life that are soul contracts we agreed to go through before being incarnated on the planet, the better we can understand that every thought coming through us is for our evolution. We can then start to move into our calling and easily say no to things instead of saying yes. We understand our mission is important in the greater scale of the universe, and we no longer get distracted by false love, validation, illusions, codependent looping, or low-level frequencies. Instead, we become laser-focused on empowering ourselves by saying no more than we say yes. We have now created the energetic space for that yes to be incredible—for our life to turn into magic, because we finally embody being a living example of *An Uncompromised Life* to our soul's truest calling, which is to live in our fullest expression so freedom can ring for us.

Go out and own your no because I know when I said no to hanging out and phone calls, and instead decided to write this book, a whole new HECK YES *Uncompromised Life* became a reality. It was better than I could have even dreamed. Now, I'm excited for the day that you choose to allow your own version of this process to take place for you.

CHAPTER 8

Believing in the Adventure of Life

I was lying in a hotel room with my parents. I had just finished watching the movie *Adrift*—the story of a woman who left San Diego right after high school. She decided to stay in Mexico for six months, but it ended up being six years. She traveled the world, and she met the love of her life. They sailed around the world together. Then one day, her partner was offered a job to sail to San Diego. She wasn't ready to return; she hadn't been back in years, ever since she had started her adventures around the world. Yet since it was a paid opportunity for them to sail on a beautiful yacht, she agreed to make the trip to return to San Diego (even though it was against what her gut was telling her to do). During the voyage, they happened to have a shipwreck, and he badly injured his leg. The woman had to do all the work to get them to land and take care of him. The movie portrayed them at sea for forty-nine days before they made it to Hawaii.

However, in Hawaii, the rescuers found only her on the boat, suggesting that she had been hallucinating since the shipwreck, which had not injured her boyfriend but killed him. However, to this day, the woman still sails the world, despite what happened, and still believes her boyfriend was with her on that boat for the final forty-nine days.

I sat there in the hotel so emotionally involved in the movie of how this woman, at age twenty-four, was able to follow her dream to sail the globe. Not a worry in the world of how it would all work out; she just trusted her heart. And that she still, to this day, travels, believing in the adventures of life even though she was drifting for forty-nine days. Now that is what it means to live *An Uncompromised Life*. To follow your heart and dreams, regardless of the experienced trauma you've went through.

The reason I was in tears over this movie was because I had left my corporate job at age twenty-three to travel the world. I followed my heart to create a world beyond my wildest dreams. Yet, I was always worried about money instead of simply enjoying the process. I obsessed over how I would be successful, instead of enjoying the dream I had chosen to pursue. When I watched this movie, I realized I had to take responsibility—to own that part of me that had missed out on being present in those moments. I had missed out on following my heart to the end of that journey, which was to truly feel, impact others, love without bounds, and believe in the truth that the adventure of life can be real for each of us.

After the movie ended, I frantically turned off the television. I tried to go to sleep, however, a multitude of thoughts kept rushing through my mind. The thoughts said that even though I had traveled the world and had done a lot of things, I had always had an underlying worry of how I was going to make money, and that worry had never gone away. Everything in my life revolved around doing things with the intention of making money, and the truth hit me with the force of a train. I thought I had done the work. I thought I had done the journaling. I thought I listened to all the podcasts and YouTube videos that were meant to help me get into a higher vibrational state. Still, it was obvious I was missing something because even while I was offering to help or connect with people, deep within me was the question, "How is this going to make me money or move me forward?" I was missing the point of just being present in life, with no attachment to some pre-conceived future outcome. I didn't fully embody believing in the adventure of life and what that could mean for me.

As I sat tossing and turning in my hotel room with my parents after celebrating Christmas, I was just coming out of being $100K in debt. I was anxious about how I was going to pay my team members the next day; yet, I had a full online business that was telling people how they could live their dreams. Was I really living my dream?

➤ I just had an unexpected pregnancy.

➤ I chose to let go of the baby.

➤ I was not sold on the Ph.D. program I was waiting to receive acceptance from.

➤ I was obsessing over a guy, and I had no clue if he liked me or not.

➤ I did not have 1:1 clients I loved.

➤ My friends were worried about me.

➤ I was not reaching my money goals.

I was also tossing and turning because it seemed that *all* of the things that could go wrong were going wrong. Financial problems, health problems, business problems, unplanned activities, relationship problems, and an unwanted pregnancy. Why was this all happening?

I closed my eyes and this question stared me in the face:

"What is it going to take for you to live a life uncompromised —one filled with your soul's truest calling?"

I realized I was missing the point of being present for the adventure of life. Instead of being present in my experiences, I was focused on how to be successful. I was compromising who I was to be liked by others. The truth is: Many of us do this unconsciously all the time, and we've done it for years (or even decades).

See: The universe is always speaking to us. The question becomes: Are we listening? In *Adrift*, this woman did not want to return home to San Diego. She initially felt she was not ready. This woman didn't listen to her true desire to *not* return home, and the love of her life died at sea while she was adrift for forty-nine days. She ended up surrendering to this experience—becoming part of the adventure of her life. She allowed herself to cope with the experience by creating a reality where he was present with her until she arrived in Hawaii. She believed she was going to live. She believed that her life had more adventures to be lived. Even though her current reality was not a very appealing adventure, and it seemed like there may be no way out, she decided to create her own adventure so that she could survive, live to tell others about it, and inspire other people to believe things will always work out.

Here is the part of the story I found fascinating: The same way this woman believed her partner was there with her on the ship for the forty-nine days is the same way I feel about Ella.

When I chose to have an abortion, it was not a fun part of my life adventure. It sucked. It was painful. When Ella's dad chose not to be there for me when I needed him, it was painful. It added to the heartbreak of my adventure. Part of my healing process in my adventure of life was for the world to show up and have a little girl tell me her name was Ella instead of her real name, Lila. It was for Ella's dad to give me a toy unicorn and say the name was El. It was for a little girl to be playing with me right before I went into the room to take the abortion pill and to tell me my grandma's best friend's name was Ella. It was the random pink card that showed up from a stranger with $245 worth of gift cards. These were all parts of my adventure of an unplanned pregnancy, choosing an abortion, and trying to understand how to cope with it all.

I believe we each have stories like this that prevail in our trauma. We have stories in our heartaches to help us on our healing journey to living *An Uncompromised Life*. These miracles that show up in the craziness of life can only happen when we face the hard truths. The reason we experience trauma is because we compromise our character. This woman in *Adrift* compromised her character by knowing she wasn't ready to return to San Diego. I compromised my character by agreeing to be in a relationship that was never going to work for me.

I truly believe before any traumatic event occurs in our life, the world gives us multiple signs and a "knowing within our gut" to not do something or stop doing something to prevent the trauma from occurring. The world desires, instead, for us to have the adventures of our dreams. From the outside looking in, it appeared I was I living my adventure to the fullest. I had been to over forty countries by age twenty-six, lived in four U.S. states by myself (not knowing anyone before moving there), and had been on amazing dates, yet the question remained: Was I present for the adventures or was I so busy worrying about how a present moment would bring me success that I missed the purpose and joy in those adventures?

I compromised parts of my true adventure stories because I was teaching about standing in your truth. Yet over time, I no longer spoke my truth. Within this story, I found myself unable to be who I was because my desire to be loved—by someone who could never truly love me because they didn't even know me—was so strong. I was selling myself short and not trusting the adventure of life. This was something I had to come to an awareness of, and I did so through this movie. This process propelled me forward—to start learning how to forgive myself.

I kept asking myself what it would take for me to finally live uncompromised, for me to live the life I preach about. As I lay there trying to fall sleep with all these thoughts screaming inside of me, I knew I needed to take action.

I committed to start by being honest with myself.

I did what I do best—write. I opened up a word document and started typing this story, for myself and for you. I figured the best way to take care of myself was to write it all out on paper—getting my thoughts out of my head and on to paper. I knew, if I could get to the place of helping and empowering myself, I could then help you.

This was me being raw, honest, and real. I had to face the fact that "fake it till you make it" was not going to work. You cannot fake happiness, you cannot fake joy, you cannot fake a true adventure. You can travel the world, you can be in a relationship, you can show up to a job, but deep down you realize you were only DOING those things to receive a certain result—you missed the whole point of believing in the gifts life's adventures can bring you. When you show up to something expecting a desired result, you lose the momentum of believing in the miracles of life's adventures. When you lose belief, you have nothing left. Regardless of what is happening in your life or has happened, you must always believe it's part of a greater adventure you do not yet know.

Then, something amazing and transformational happened. I realized I cared more about the process of writing this book instead of obsessing over the result this book would bring.

Most of us (including myself) become worried about how everything will work out—how the money will come, when the boat will save us, if we can trust ourselves to sail again, if we can allow ourselves to love again, if we can forgive ourselves for lying. Well, when we go into this analytical state it blocks us from being able to believe in the miraculous adventures that still await us in life. Because as I shared in Chapter 6, we cannot solve emotional problems with logic. Instead, we must learn to trust and believe that whatever is going on in our life in this moment is part of the life adventure we are meant to endure for our highest good.

To truly live *An Uncompromised Life*, you must commit to believing that everything you have experienced or will experience in your life is part of the adventure. It is to trust that your life can be extraordinary right now.

To live *An Uncompromised Life* means to surrender, in every moment, to whatever life reveals and to become one with the adventure of your heart's desire, trusting that you are here for a greater good. Instead of losing focus and becoming distracted by what an experience, person, or thing can bring into your life, you can live *An Uncompromised Life* by releasing all subconscious attachments to how money will show up, how friends will show up, how people might support you, and instead, focus on the adventure life is bringing to you in every moment. Because all we have is the here and now within the adventure of life.

Just like the woman in *Adrift* and my beautiful story of how the name Ella came to me, surrender to the truth that life is giving you an adventure. Believe that in every moment—through death, through trauma, through amazing memories—that you can live *An Uncompromised Life* and that the best adventures are still waiting for you to experience them in this life.

A perfect example of this: Before I went to bed after writing this chapter to you, I prayed a prayer to God and said please provide me with a miracle to know I am on the right path. The next morning, after writing my feelings out as the start of this book, I woke up to the first two sales from a Facebook ad I had been running.

My mouth dropped.

I thought, "No way!"

Did I just write about believing in the adventure of life, having no attachment to what this would mean to the bottom line, and God opened the door for two random sales to come through as an indication that I was on the right path?

"I think the world did just gave me a confirmation that I should keep surrendering to the adventure of life, trusting what I am feeling, acting on it, and stop overanalyzing how it is all going to work out." I started believing that writing this book and sharing my story was part of my life adventure.

Well to add to this, later that morning after I made these two sales, I had plans to go to the spa. I heard the voice of the universe come through me, telling me to bring my laptop with me to the spa. I was having breakfast overlooking the mountains in Arizona and I heard the voice of God tell me to open my laptop and start writing to finish this chapter. With excitement I opened my laptop to finish writing this chapter. This is really how the world works when you believe in the adventures that life can provide if you choose to be present, with no attachment or pre-conceived ideas, and with no focus on the results (particularly the financial ones).

As I typed throughout that day, I realized that our souls always have the opportunity to go deeper into living *An Uncompromised Life*. Everything that exists around us—whether it's a tree, a window allowing you to see the sunlight or moonlight, or your neighbor walking outside—everything always holds a greater depth of beauty to be seen and experienced.

No matter who we are, we are always going to crave that next adventure. The woman in *Adrift* never stopped sailing the world. We shouldn't stop either. There is something beautiful our souls are craving for us to see and experience right where we are. We just have to take one step at a time, one breath at a time, and one moment at a time, slowing down enough to realize the beauty that exists right in front of us.

An Uncompromised Life does not happen with a million dollars, a single vacation, or with a committed relationship. *An Uncompromised Life* happens when all of the small moments in life accumulate, taking us on a journey. *An Uncompromised Life* is when we are content with not knowing what is coming next—how we're going to smile, how we're going to pay our bills, or how we're going to plan for retirement. It's when we don't focus on being the perfect mom or the Rockstar partner. It's when we don't worry about how we're going to get over a death or traumatic experience.

An Uncompromised Life unfolds when we empower our-selves to believe that there is a greater meaning and message for us in every life experience, regardless of if we perceive the experiences as bad or good. When we don't waste our time worrying about figuring it out ourselves, because we have a trust in the universe that the answers we seek from any and all experiences will come naturally and when they are meant to come to us.

Life's mini adventures are what make the destination worth it. When you end up with your last moments on this earth, you will care so little about the results and so much more about the adventures that brought you the result. So stop worrying and get moving.

CHAPTER 9

Becoming a Heart-Centered Business Leader

L esson number eight is the most grounding and crucial gift I have received in learning to live *An Uncompromised Life*. The truth is we all have extremely painful and traumatic stories that have broken our hearts beyond belief. So, I became curious about what it is that prevents people from getting over a broken heart and what empowers people to heal themselves so darn fast—fast enough that others wonder how in the world they ever overcame such traumatic, unspeakable things? What I have learned to be true is: The moment you turn your trauma into a purpose-driven business, your life changes wildly fast. I've seen the moment someone focuses their pain into becoming a heart-centered business leader; that is what consistently heals your life so fast that people wonder how in the world you did it.

I heard of a woman who experienced a horrific trauma. Four men forced her to watch as they raped and killed her family. Yet until the day they of their death sentences, she went and visited these four men every day in prison to pray with them and help them on their journey to forgiving themselves for what they had done. She became a speaker, and eventually, created a business for herself helping others who went through similar trauma.

This woman's trauma was so deep that she knew the only way she could heal herself and live *An Uncompromised Life* was to feel as if she helped these men heal from the awful pain they must have experienced to do such a painful thing to someone else. However, visiting with these men was where her most important and rapid healing journey occurred. She had to find a way to make sense of why this happened, and the only way she could do that was by helping these men understand why they were capable of doing such a thing. Whatever the trauma or pain is, the healing journey begins when you become a heart-centered leader and it then becomes your business. You make a lifestyle out of the trauma, instead of living in a false matrix that wasn't designed for you.

Remember: The evil things people do is not because something randomly happens overnight. I don't believe people are evil; they just have been trained and programmed for decades, typically since childhood, to remove their feelings, ignore their hearts, and do toxic things. They had evil done to them, and they are simply acting out what they were taught.

I used to ask Ella's dad, "What does love feel like to you? What does falling in love mean to you?"

His reply: "You always ask questions that lead to no real conversation."

Now, Ella's dad is by no means evil. His answer simply revealed his capacity around love, which he learned from his childhood. When you remember this, you can show compassion for the people you have allowed to hurt you, because they simply don't know any better. However, this doesn't mean you allow them in your life.

As I've shared previously, I believe we chose and continue to choose this life. So when toxic dysfunction occurs in our life, we must start to become curious about why this experience was attracted to us—through a frequency or completion of a karmic debt and/or soul contract. From that place of becoming curious, becoming a heart-centered business leader becomes available for us. We will start to see the problems we have in our life and how we can create solutions for them to heal our own lives, which then empowers us to offer solutions to help others. That is all a heart-centered business leader is: simply solving problems that help enhance the lives of others.

I have worked with many people—from rape victims to refugees who have been branded my men, male prisoners to cancer survivors, divorcees to receivers of narcissistic abuse, alcoholics to drug addicts, those who have lost children, and the list can go on. I have interacted with someone from every type of trauma you can imagine, and this is what I know to be true: The people who break through and heal the fastest are those who turn their trauma and "victimhood" into a heart-centered business. These people realize that they are not the only ones who are suffering from depression, abuse, addiction, or codependency, and they want to take action to do something about it to make the world a better place.

It is in this process—that someone raises their hand and says I am going to act with courage, look at my own self, understand how I can move through this trauma, and become better so I can help other people who are in a similar situation—that you rapidly heal yourself. This is when you become the person who no longer suffers for a lifetime; you become the hero that many look up to. Usually these types of people create more wealth and success than one could ever imagine. The irony is: These heart-centered leaders and purpose-driven entrepreneurs never started out with the intent to make money. They started out because they were genuinely suffering, they had no one to turn to, yet they were committed to healing themselves, and then other people starting asking them for help. They became a somewhat self-made holistic healing doctor from their trauma—putting one foot in front of the other, which eventually led to a whole business that is helping so many people going through a similar trauma the victim once went through.

Without my crystals, this book, loving support from a few friends, and the unexplainable signs from the universe, I wouldn't have recovered from such a crazy relationship, created a better relationship with my parents, and overcome the loss of a child. It was through me creating something new that I was able to release the negativity and see that everything was for a greater purpose. This allowed me to turn the sadness into gratitude. Every time we can move to gratitude, our life shifts drastically.

In writing this book, I embodied a deeper layer of a heart-centered business leader, and it was another tool—a resource—I could add to my business. However, here is a huge key: I did not write this book for the sole intent *to* increase sales in my business. I wrote this book for my own healing and to help others who felt alone, isolated, and had no idea where to turn for help from a child loss and overcoming heart-break. That is when you naturally become a heart-centered business leader without having to force yourself or exert so much effort.

It was in this process when I started to do my own research on narcissism and started to write down my emotions, that I started to let go, and come into a place of peace. I was then okay to authentically share with people—shortly and one-by-one—what happened in my life. I slowly admitted I let go of Ella instead of saying I had a miscarriage. I began to share that I help people find purpose from their trauma. My business started to increase, my clients became more aligned with the way I saw the world, and my programs started selling on their own. I had so many ideas coming through me all the time (the natural laws of the universe). My life began to shift and heal rapidly; it took less than five months from the moment I let go of Ella and two months with no contact with Ella's dad for me to truly build this huge, solid foundation to living *An Uncompromised Life.*

It wasn't easy, though. During that five-month period, there were days and nights when I could not stop crying. There were times I thought I would rather be in anyone else's body but mine. Somehow, I always came back to knowing I had to figure this out for myself and for a greater, collective healing. I had to do this to help others be able to find their Ella's in the midst of unexplainable trauma. Even deeper, I knew I had to do the healing for myself—so Ella could truly be free. I realized if I didn't take this journey of healing for Ella, I would be repeating the same generational pattern. At first, I wanted to make the crystals and tell the story of Ella—in remembrance of her. Then, I remembered—I had to do this for me alone. I had to choose myself and rise up, be there for myself, become my own best friend, and become my own business advisor and consultant . . . for me. Because it was only when I decided to do it for *me* that I was able to truly set Ella free, set myself free, and empower others with various traumas to be guided to find self-healing through a chapter from my life.

As mentioned in Chapter 3, when we start to live in alignment with who we are meant to be, the laws of the universe allow all of the business ideas to creatively flow through you—so you can see what resources you can create to solve people's problems. For me, I knew this book was a start, then an audio book would be next, and maybe an online program or community to help the other men and women suffering like I did on the nights when I was crying on the floor. I knew others would benefit from learning I had tough moments, such as when I screamed, "I cannot have his baby!" I knew I had to create something to help others make sense of life and take control of their emotional well-being, finances, and their ability to help others heal. Yet deep down, I knew it had to start with me. I knew that doing it for me would allow me to show up to help others. I knew if I stayed broken—a victim and depressed—there was no way I could be available to create a business to guide others to *An Uncompromised Life*.

I have learned why becoming a heart-centered business leader is such an important lesson: We need more businesses in all different industries. Each trauma opens the door for a new product or solution to be birthed. For example: different cancers need different solutions, different addictions need different solutions, different heart-breaks need various solutions. We cannot do this mission alone, creating uncompromised lives for others. I haven't faced every trauma, so I need you to rise up and live your own version of *An Uncompromised Life*, creating your heart-centered business so you can help people through the specific trauma you have been through. (By the way, we have all been through some type of trauma, and if you say you have not, then you are either in denial or using an avoidance strategy to protect yourself.)

I know the moment you decide to help other people and see you can build a business around it, your life will change drastically. I have developed eight golden rules that you can implement—so you can create this heart-centered business without feeling overwhelmed, stressed, or anxious. I know one thing to be true about purpose-driven businesses: The ones who succeed have so much fun along the way, enjoy the journey, and truly love meeting every single person they encounter so they can educate others on how to overcome anything and live *An Uncompromised Life.*

Here are the Eight Golden Rules to becoming a heart-centered business leader:

1. **Following Your Obsessive Knowing (also known as Intuition)**

    This simply means that you get still enough to hear your inner voice, guiding you and telling you the exact action step to take. To call that friend, ask for a loan from the bank, put that website page up, go to the networking event, go on that date. This is the voice that is guiding you to take action to create your own freedom, so you can then impact others. Most times it makes no logical sense, yet it just feels so right.

2. **Transition from "My Career" to Growth of Others Lives**

    This means you stop focusing on the victimhood of your trauma and see how it can impact others. You stop making this about poor little you and see it as a greater collective healing. This is about you seeing how this can lead to other people changing their lives. Yes, you can create a business by empowering others to invest in their education or products that would change their life. Think about whatever you are going to create—how much money would you have paid to have that guide, education, or tool kit when you were suffering? Probably way more than you are going to charge. Stop thinking about you, take action, and know you can help others!

3. Change Your Language to Change the World

The way you talk to yourself changes everything. For example, I rarely use the word *abortion* when talking about my actions. Instead, I say I chose to *let go of* Ella. This empowers me—it guides me to cope with what happened because Ella and I did this together. It was what was best for me—to kill my disease of people pleasing and truly save her life, shifting the generational lineage. From this place, it was much easier to create this book. It allowed me to dissolve shame and judgement much quicker, in addition to allowing me to take action and add this to my existing business, empowering others. The language we use is either empowering us or hurting us—it's up to you to decide how you want to talk to yourself so you can either take action or remain a victim.

4. The Power of Choice

Everything in our life is created by us. As I've shared, there are no accidents; our choices accumulate over time and either create something great or something not-so-great. However, in every moment we can choose to recreate our life. I believe in every moment we can choose to start a business, impact people, and grow an income—from a heart-centered space. This way we choose to leave a legacy and impact people many lifetimes after us to come, because we choose to rise up over whatever perceived injustice occurred to us. From this place of empowered choice, we naturally create a business, opportunities, and clients we love.

5. **Fall in Love with No**

In order to heal, we must learn to say no. You can no longer be the 1-800 hotline for everyone to call. You must say no to people pulling energy from you and instead redirect them to a website, products, or resources you have created for them to receive relief. You will have to learn to be okay with the fact that you may not be able to help every person individually, yet you can still help one by one through your products. You must say no, so you can create systems and processes that allow you to impact more people. Otherwise you will stay stuck in the same pattern, repeating the same trauma because you are being a slave to helping everyone else before yourself.

6. **Alignment Trumps Everything**

In order for a heart-centered business to work, you have to have embodied all the other lessons in *An Uncompromised Life* before becoming a heart-centered leader. You must be so committed to being in alignment with yourself, feeling good about being you, and being alone instead of falling for false illusions of safety, validation, company, happiness, and success. Otherwise your business will have massive failures that could cause it not to make it. The purpose driven businesses that always impact the most people are those that stay in alignment with the reason they desire to impact others, remembering they are creating something they wish they had when they went through the trauma.

7. **Replace Distractions with Vision**

Every person, situation, and object that takes you away from your alignment must be replaced with the vision. For example, I knew long before Ella was birthed that Ella's dad was a distraction, yet I didn't listen. However, I also had to go through that so in the future when men come into my life, I will choose my business over them, because a man will not provide for me like my business of impacting others will. Whatever your distractions are, you must become more committed to the vision that you can absolutely help tons of people by simply being you.

8. **Become the Identity of the Future You Now**

In order to become a purpose-driven business and succeed, you must start to study other leaders you admire. You must start to see what leadership characteristics you admire, and you must bring that into your identity. You are going to totally have to shift from the choices that created the mess you are in, in order to become the man or woman you are meant to become. For you to believe you can create a business, for you to know you can help yourself and guide others through healing, you must become a new person. Start to think like this new person, start to talk like this new person, start to take action like a person who is living a life uncompromised to your heart's true desires. Now this is a leader that people will look up to and admire. Yet even more importantly, you will become the person that saved your own self, and you are going to help a lot more people's lives become easier when getting over their trauma. Because in the process of healing yourself, you create a space for others to come and heal without having to do it all alone.

This is what it takes to heal yourself, leave a legacy, and become a heart-centered business leader who is worth learning from and remembering, yet more importantly, this is what it takes to complete your own circle of karmic debt and pass on better DNA to the lineage that is to come after you. There is no greater reward than looking yourself in the mirror and saying, "I did it. I became the person I always dreamed about, and I did it from my heart and soul. I didn't sell myself to the devil. I didn't compromise my soul just to get money; I created the path for others to have easier lives." From this place, congratulations! You just initiated a new level of consciousness and awareness into your being. From this place, I meet you in the infinite cosmic world because you just conquered and earned a truly uncompromised life, and no one can take that healing journey or your rise to the top away from you.

I truly believe, no matter what you have gone through, that once you allow yourself to become available to become a heart-centered leader, you will naturally start receiving action steps how you can create your own purpose-driven business, or become part of a business where you utilize the skillsets you gained through your trauma to help others, you will live *An Uncompromised Life.*

CHAPTER 10

Owning Your Power

L et's talk about the power of innocence as it relates to owning your power. The innocence of acting in love and engaging in playful interactions are two of the greatest assets we each possess. Yet at the same time, they also bring heartache. New love and playfulness bring so many beautiful lessons, if we choose to see them. The lesson here, number nine on my list, is that you must care about you before you can care about anybody else; otherwise the power you hold within you and the value you bring to the table will be used, abused, and unappreciated. When we are in our divinity of being innocent and unaware of what is happening in the world, when we are unconsciously indulging in play as I was with Ella's dad, this is exactly what causes traumatic experiences in our life.

Here is a string of examples. In our innocence, when we decide to routinely answer phone calls from that one friend who always has a problem, it compounds overtime, and we devalue our time and knowledge, giving them away to a friend who is not choosing to get out of his or her own way and circumstances. When we unconsciously buy clothes that are made by women and children in inhumane working conditions, overtime, through our innocence of simply buying clothes, we contribute to someone else's poor health and unjust life, instead of choosing to only buy brands that take a strong stand against those injustices. Over time, when you commit to only buying clothes that are vegan friendly and from companies that have verified manufacturing facilities, that is when you start owning the value of your true power. No longer are you just doing something, receiving something, or offering something in ignorance, you are aligning yourself and taking actions that show you are someone with poise, respect, power, and values.

When you act in pure innocence and play, choosing to be unaware of just how powerful you are to the greater collective healing, you create a compromised life, as well as unconscious damage to yourself and other people, which is exactly why Ella came to be. In this lesson, I want to shed light on ways we subconsciously dim our light, devalue ourselves, and disown our power.

When we were all little kids, we just wanted to play. At some point in my journey, I missed maturing childlike play into purposeful play. I think many of us do this because we decide to allow anyone into our lives who we think understands us, or will simply listen to us. From that point, when we feel like someone understands us, we share all of our life, knowledge, skillsets, and talents with people because we finally feel like we are not alone—like a little kid playing in a sandbox. When we feel a connection, we can begin to compromise ourselves if we yet have not found a stable and grounded connection within ourselves. Part of writing this book is to teach you through my own life that giving ourselves away freely to others because we feel a moment of connection (when we do not have a true connection within ourselves yet) usually doesn't work out well.

Most of my life I was not owning my power; instead, I was irresponsibly giving my power away at the cost of my own wellbeing. I remember when I was little—and even at times in college—hanging out with people I didn't even like because it felt better than the pain I felt when I was alone with myself. Every time you answer the phone, hang out with someone, or even have an interaction with someone, you are exchanging energy and value. If we just go out and give our energy away to everyone freely, we are not going to have a lot of energy left to focus on what we really want to focus on—we are going to be exhausted from being everyone else's lifeline. This results in us totally devaluing ourselves as humans, giving our power away, and wasting our precious time on things that will not create tangible returns from our time. This unconscious mindset and unawareness is very dangerous. We create a lifestyle—pretending we are "innocent" to the evils of the world and that we are seemingly "doing" the right thing, such as hanging out with "the" friends, instead of honoring ourselves and doing what is best for us and for everyone else—and we lose the purity of our innocence.

Think about this: If you know someone is an alcoholic, and they call and ask you to buy them alcohol or drive them to the store, are you going to do it? Hopefully not, otherwise you'd be an enabler, allowing their problem and their health to worsen. You would be devaluing the power you hold as a human if you allowed yourself to play this game with someone. Well, the same is true when you allow yourself to show up to events you do not want to be at, when you answer the same call to the same friend who always has problems, or you share your gifts and knowledge with every single person you meet when they yet have not shown you they are committed to staying in your life. In reality, you are overextending yourself, so there ends up being nothing left of you *for you*. This devalues you, because if you are not taking care of yourself, there is no possible way you can take care of other people.

There was one significant action step I took in my life, which changed my life tremendously and helped me understand my value. Our brains have been wired a certain way up until this point. Our brains have created a beautiful mechanism that has allowed us to survive and get to the point we are at.

I was having obsessive thoughts about what everyone else thought, what everyone else did, what people would think of me if I said no, and so on. I came to understand all the other lessons I have talked about in this book, yet my obsessive thoughts were leading me to struggle with identifying the value I brought as a person. Afterall, I was trained to be so focused on everyone else.

So I went to a healer and shared this with her, and she said the neurons in my brain may not be firing correctly, and she suggested I get neurofeedback therapy. I took her up on this, and I went to get tested to find out what was going on in my beautiful brain. The results came back, and my IQ is on the level of a genius, yet my brain was totally unstable. I suffered from extreme anxiety, fatigue, PTSD, depression, ADHD, OCD, and I had no sense of self. I had trouble putting thoughts into language, and at times, I would go into robotic-like states because I couldn't understand emotionally what was going on around me, so my coping mechanism was to leave my body. At times I just did things with no emotion.

Why did this happen?

It was the result of extreme trauma I suffered as a child, being diagnosed with cancer, and my intuitive abilities to pick up on others' energy. As a coping mechanism to avoid complete depression or unstable emotional places where I couldn't function, my brain shut itself off from having emotions at all. This enabled me to still function as a human being, even if it was just in a robotic-state to get me through life.

When I found this out, I remember thinking, "WOW! This is incredible—our brain knows how to protect us so we can survive." Then I wondered, "How many other people have a brain that is functioning as a way for them to survive because of past trauma? Surely if this happened to me, there must be other people out there operating with a brain that is helping them cope with life, working purely on survival mode because of unhealed trauma." I imagined there might be millions of people with brains that are set up to compromise their lives because their brains are not firing their neurons correctly from past traumas. Our brains' job is to make sure we survive, not thrive.

After the initial neurofeedback assessment, I realized that to live out my potential and value, I must invest my money in the things that would empower me to live my best life. Even though I didn't have the money for this, I just said yes, trusting the money would show up, which it did (Chapter 3—natural laws of the universe). My thirteen weeks of neurofeedback therapy, shifted my whole life rapidly because I created the space I needed to take my power back. I began to communicate openly and honestly with people. Then, those people could guide me to other people until I found the right help for me. It is in honoring your power (and honing in on it) that we discover what it is we need in order to access deeper layers of our power . . . and we actually become more powerful! It is in our vulnerability that we take ownership of our power, so we can become who we are meant to be.

Along with owning your power, it's important to value your money. How many times have we paid for something when we haven't been happy with the service? How many times have we felt like someone sold us something and then underdelivered? Yet, we said nothing. We simply let people rob from us or steal from us when we knew deep down, we did not feel good about the value exchange of money—what we paid for did not match what we received.

A personal example is when I allowed mentors or friends to use sales tactics against me—knowing my very weakness of needing validation, having low self-worth, and wanting to feel accepted. So before I knew it, I was involved in more mentorship packages and programs than I knew what to do with. The reality is: I didn't need their services. I knew that and they knew that. However, my need for connection with people was so deep that I was willing to do anything to find that connection, even if it meant disregarding my values, denying what I truly needed to be successful in business, throwing money at things, and dismissing opportunities to speak my truth. As a result, I devalued myself and lost some of the power within me. Yet, I had to go through this in order to complete a soul contract for my greatest evolution.

However, let me tell you about the first time I started to take the power back in regards to my money and how I started to understand the value that I could bring to others. I want you to see how easy this can be. I had hired a woman for $25,000 to fly from Australia to LA to do a branding shoot and completely redo my online brand. Well, this woman forgot her luggage at the airport, did not know anything about LA, and invited another woman to come and stay at the Airbnb for free. She kept crying because she felt like she was not pleasing me, some of my shoes and clothes arrived late, the sizes of clothes were wrong, there were no receipts of the clothes that were bought, the videographer was split between both of us, and the pricing was always changing. I ended up leaving a few days early, and she made me split the Airbnb evenly after I left.

On top of that, she posted my branded photos on Facebook without my approval, and because the photoshoot had been an absolute mess, I never even used the photos.

The whole situation was a total loss of my value and power. I handed so much trust over to this woman to take care of details for me because had no idea what I truly desired, and I expected her to have answers for things I didn't have answers to myself. How often do we do this—trust someone with our money before doing the proper research to see if it's even in alignment? I'd guess often. We do this because we are not acknowledging our power yet. We are not seeing the value we bring to someone by offering them the opportunity to receive our money. We bring value to people by bringing them our problems to solve, and we keep them in business.

After this mess of a situation happened, I decided this was the last time I would be screwed over financially. I used my voice, and I used it in a big way. There was no way I was going to let this person steal my money by doing a crappy job. There were parts where I overpaid, and I asked for a break-out sheet of all the expenses, along with a refund. Regarding the breakout sheet—it took days to get, and the numbers were not correct. I ended up getting two refunds, and still feel I should have received more money back. However, the point is that it was the first time I had stood up to someone who was stealing from me—consciously or unconsciously, it doesn't matter. I did not have boundaries in place that helped me demand amazing service for what I was paying. However, the moment I left the Airbnb early and used my voice to fight for every penny I believed I was owed, that is when I started to see my value. I started getting what I had demanded. This can absolutely happen for you, as well, when you start to own your value by using your voice to express your needs and desires.

Another portion in owning your power is understanding when you value others over yourself. This takes on many forms. One instance may be when we constantly look at others and think they are doing a better job than we can do, so we promote them before we promote ourselves. For example, I have used Instagram in my business for over two years, and I never did a video or post promoting my own first book, *Live Your Truth*, which is about how I overcame cancer and saw that I could live my purpose and monetize it. Well, a friend of mine also released a book, and I did a testimonial video for her on my Instagram. Afterwards, I realized I had not valued my own work enough to do a video testimonial on my book, *Live Your Truth*. I was always so busy sharing everyone else's work and honoring what they were doing that I never saw the value I already brought to the table. This type of behavior leads us to live a compromised life. In my innocence of always promoting other people, being there for other people, and doing everything for everyone except myself, I was left exhausted, angry, and resentful. In my false idea of relationships, I was helping everyone else; yet, I was causing more problems for myself because I was sharing others' work while not sharing my own. It is only you who can set yourself free—by choosing you and realizing just how important you are to the greater equation of collective healing. Because you cannot live *An Uncompromised Life* if you choose everyone else over yourself.

The last message I want to share with you within this lesson is for you to start owning your power is understanding how your emotions are guiding you to a massive breakthrough. When you feel frustrated, angry, or annoyed with anyone, you are living a compromised life—putting too much effort into someone who is influencing and impacting your mood.

Remember when Ella's dad said he had visions of me dying or a silver pole going through my head? I was angry, yet in reality I had to see that I couldn't place this emotion on him. I had to take responsibility for devaluing myself to such a place where I allowed someone into my life who would envision such a thing. It's in us not having self-worth that we attract such a low point experience in our life. It was from that place I knew if I didn't get him out of my life that his visions would have eventually become reality.

It was in that moment I took my power back and I asked myself, "Am I going to keep a guy in my life who has visions of me dying?"

The only answer I had was, "Heck no!"

It was in this new awareness of committing to myself that I deserved better, I started to fight for myself and my values. I chose to no longer allow myself to accept low-level friends, business partnerships, integrity, and character traits. I started to realize that I bring value to the table, and I deserve quality value in return.

Within this beautiful tragedy was a lesson for me to go through for my highest evolution and growth so I could begin to live *An Uncompromised Life*. It was in that moment of taking my power back that I birthed my "Colleen Gallagher Podcast," became more fit, committed to yoga, showed up for my business differently, changed the conversations with my friends, started eating healthier, started saying no, started consistently fighting for my money, honored my needs, and realized my time is valuable. It was within this that I found my power, so I am forever grateful, and I hope that in these lessons and stories I shared in this chapter, you choose to own your power and start to discover how incredible you are.

Only you can choose—at any and every moment—to take your power back and understand where you compromised yourself. It is only when you become aware of why you are compromising yourself that you will stop allowing yourself to make excuses for others who are not treating you the way you deserve to be treated, and stop forcing yourself into situations that do not empower you. I encourage you to take your power back and live a life that is uncompromised to you. For the first time in your life, you'll feel what it's like to put yourself first instead of putting yourself on the backburner.

As I learned from my mum, who put me before herself in everything—I was her purpose, and I was her source of power. It's beautiful, yet at the same time, it allowed me to embody the very habits and traits that guided me to ignoring myself and receiving an unplanned pregnancy.

By you being here, reading this book, you are opening yourself up to understanding just how important it is to choose yourself, avoid giving your power away so freely, and honor yourself. You never know who is watching you and looking up to you as an example of whom they want to become. My hope is that you practice taking your power back and choosing yourself in the small moments, because those add up to the big, beautiful moments of *An Uncompromised Life*.

CHAPTER 11

Falling In Love

Deep down, all of us are hopeless romantics. We all want to be swept off our feet—taken away on a huge love adventure that turns into a beautiful life together with challenging moments where we grow together and exciting moments where we expand together. Lesson ten is about falling in love.

I've been the kind of woman who until Ella typically I dated multiple people at once—very non-committal – yet the relationships were deep, intense and fast. I have always been married to my career or purpose, except for the three occasions when I was in more serious relationships.

The day I learned I was pregnant was the day that completely changed my idea of what it means to fall in love. I no longer cared about falling in love with a person. I wanted to fall in love with life.

- ➤ I wanted to fall in love with how my alarm clock goes off.
- ➤ I wanted to fall in love with how I press snooze or shoot up out of bed.
- ➤ I wanted to fall in love with walking slowly and feeling the air pass through me.
- ➤ I wanted to fall in love with the way I looked into someone's eyes.
- ➤ I wanted to fall in love with every little detail about my life.

This is much different than what relationship coaches tell you—to fall in love with yourself first (self-love).

I believe that everything around us is simply a reflection of what is going on within us. Clearly, becoming pregnant was something I did not want, and it happened because internally, I was forcing myself to do things that compromised the nature of my character and what I desired. Many women have trouble forgiving themselves for letting go of a child; instead, I made the commitment to my child when I let her go that I would no longer compromise myself for love. From that moment, I was determined to decide how I could fall in love with the whole experience, so I wouldn't remain a victim of my own life.

Let's bring it full circle here. In that moment when I screamed out, "I cannot have his baby!" I asked myself this important question, which I think we all should do in our painful moments: "How can I find love in this moment?"

When I closed my eyes and started to breathe, taking myself back to that moment, I can see the woman handing me the pill, I can see her compassion, and I can see the honest admiration she had for my courage to do what was right for me. I see her acknowledging the beauty in me, even though I was only experiencing pain in that moment. It is when I create this meditation for myself—going back and observing myself in the moment of letting my child go—that I realized I am capable of seeing all the beautiful things about me in my darkest moment. (By the way, we are all capable of doing this.) When this happened, this was the first time I was seeing myself through someone else's eyes, instead of my own. It was the first time I was seeing how other beautiful people saw me, even though I could never see myself that way.

I realized, if I could just learn to fall in love with myself—by borrowing the way everyone else around me was seeing me—that maybe my life could shift. I went deeper into the idea that asked, "What if it wasn't about falling in love with me? What if it was about slowing down enough to notice all the experiences that are constantly happening around me?" Then I became more curious and started asking deeper questions, like, "What if I actually created everything around me, so I could experience love more deeply?" From the unplanned pregnancy to the unhealthy relationship, from the crystals to the name Ella coming to me three sperate times, the random card that was delivered to me, having my first meeting with my therapist ironically planned after day one of my abortion, all of this was simply something I created as a soul contract so I could understand that it wasn't about falling in love with a person—this all happened to teach me how to fall in love with life through heartbreak.

With this lesson, life just became a whole lot easier. Our ultimate dream of being hopeless romantics can come true for us in every moment. Because every moment is something we already agreed to go through, we can choose to see the good and fall in love with it. We never have to suffer in the pain for long, we are meant to fall in love with the pain, grow through it, and experience deeper emotional connections in life. Without the pain we cannot grow.

Without Ella, I wouldn't have known it's possible for me to become a mom. I wouldn't have understood how amazing it is to become a mother or the amazing love that is birthed from that role. Without Ella, I couldn't have understood what it means to choose myself. Without Ella, I couldn't have come to the awakening that we are not meant to fall in love with a person, but instead life itself. Without Ella and this whole situation, I couldn't have understood the pain my mum must have gone through to just want to be acknowledged that she was greatest mom she could be for me.

We do not need someone else in order for us to truly fall in love. Falling in love starts by making the empowered decision to first love ourselves, in our own divinity, and to then fall in love with all the small moments of everything occurring around us all the time.

Living a life that is uncompromised to your soul means you get to remember that at every moment, you can choose to make an empowered decision that will either guide you to fall more in love with life or cause you to disempower yourself and create a separation. It's a disparity between you and the reality you see in your life and how they aren't in your total control.

I had to learn through this painful journey that I could fall in love with all of it. I fell in love with Ella; I fell in love with my pregnancy and with every single person involved, because it guided me to the deeper understanding that so many of us are searching to be accepted, to be understood, and to live a life where we feel free to express ourselves.

Up until Ella, I had fallen in love with the wrong things in life. After having cancer at a young age, I just wanted to fall in love with someone. I wanted to know before I died that I understood what being in love felt like. I wanted to have a love that would take us around the world, lead us to own companies together, and have a family.

This is a false illusion of what it means to be in love, because from this ideology of falling in love, we are hoping for people to "get us." We are seeking to find the perfect person to create a home with. Yet, the reality is: Everything you desire and more exists right now for you to fall in love with. You do not need someone else to show you the way.

Ella came through me to teach me what falling in love means. It means that whatever is going on in your life right now, you—first and foremost—must choose yourself over everything. Secondly, you allow your beautiful eyes to see the world and then create beautiful thoughts in your mind, which allows you to see that everything around you wants to give you love. The question becomes, "Are you in a place to receive it?" Because if you are not in love with yourself, there is no way you can receive love from another person.

Falling in love means loving all of the experiences you chose to go through before you incarnated on this earth. It means realizing that you can be understood by the world as soon as you understand yourself.

What I have learned is: Falling in love means loving all the beautiful things around me and realizing that those things are reflections of me. I don't have to find a home in other people; I can find a piece of home wherever I feel safe, worthy, and free to be me—no matter where I am. I offer this shift in perspective because it is what guided me to know that the ability to fall in love is available to each of us in every moment—at deeper and deeper levels—and that is when another layer of *An Uncompromised Life* becomes unlocked for you.

The moment I left my corporate job in New Zealand to start my journey to travel the world, hoping to find home within it, I remember being on the phone with a friend, sharing about my hope to find this truth—love always wins.

Through my story, I hope to offer you the lesson that love truly is the most powerful force on the planet, and that home is not a place—it is found within the soul of yourself first. Then, you can co-create your sacred space with other souls on the planet.

What I've learned is: We can fall in love at every moment. We can fall in love with the soul of a stranger, the soul of a child, the soul of a neighborhood, or the soul of the food that makes up our meals and goes into our tummies. However, falling in love in the present moment cannot be intellectualized; it cannot be described; it is simply a feeling that can be felt. As soon as you put language to the feeling, you lose the frequency of the emotion.

The true moment of falling in love with life happens when you least expect it. Moments of falling in love happen when you're screaming in pain before you take an abortion pill, because you realize how resilient and strong you are. Moments of falling in love happen when you're lying on a lounge bed on a rooftop talking about the galactic universe. Moments of falling in love happen when you are at the store, and you see a loved one look at a box of pasta, and for whatever reason you find them attractive in that moment. Moments of falling in love happen when you miss your flight, and the random airport coffee person strikes up a conversation with you. Moments of falling in love happen when you cross the street, and an attractive man or woman honks at you.

Moments of falling in love happen in the way we would least expect them to happen, yet they happen all the time.

What allowed me to save myself through this awful heartbreak of a relationship and the loss of the child was choosing to allow love in. I chose to allow myself to fall in love with the clouds in the sky, the way crystals would talk to me, the way my friends would show up for me, the way my food tasted so delicious, the way my tears fell from my face and would drip onto my heart, and the way that I played with my own hair to calm my nerves.

Falling in love is the only thing that truly saved me. For so long in my healing process, I was looking to Ella's dad for comfort. I was looking to completely fall in love with him, hoping to see I had made the wrong decision in letting Ella go. I was hoping (at a subconscious level) for him to show up in the way I desired love to exist. I was hoping maybe a few years would pass, and we could try again . . . and it would all work out. I was looking for love in the wrong place, which kept causing me to suffer because he was only showing me every reason why I had made the right decision—for me to let go of the child—because it would have never been the relationship dynamic I wanted to raise a child in.

Ella's dad and I would only be capable of having love for short moments, because the operating system we both function in are in two different planes. Yet those moments of being in love we did share, I cherish. Because in those moments I felt at home within the world in an unexplainable and undeniable way. I felt like my heart bursted into a zillion white little orbs that blasted me into experiencing life through this intercon- nected cosmic universe. In those moments I felt like I lived in a fantasy world where no time or space existed, it felt like my soul entered into this portal of frequencies, where just the true essence of who I am and who he is existed. All the variables of our life, the infrastructure, the distractions dissolved away. The only thing that mattered was looking into those squiggly black eyes and receiving this divine knowing that I found the comfort of home co-created with him.

Yet what I just shared with you is rare, yet it is easy because falling in love just for a moment still allows you to escape back into reality. To really create a life that is last- ing, sustainable, fulfilling, rewarding and just simply over the top so that you fall in love over and over and over again requires honesty, commitment, effort, communication and the willingness to allow your human walls down and show the raw, vulnerable and authentic soul that truly exist within you. When you can practice being in your rawness that is when true beauty is birthed.

So, from this, I cannot honestly say that every moment in the relationship was bad or evil; there were very beautiful moments. It was those beautiful moments that kept me in an addictive, narcissistic abuse cycle—turning a blind eye and a deaf ear to the not-so-great parts. As you've learned, I co-created the beautiful moments as well as the darkness. There is never blame on anyone else, because we always co-create every experience into our life.

However, those moments of beauty we did share, I am grateful for. They showed me everything love is not. They showed me what a false illusion of love looks like when dark forces are coming through. I knew from the beginning of the relationship something was off, especially after his misleading communication of not sharing he was living with and in a relationship with at least one other woman that did not want a child. Yet, I didn't listen to this and allowed the darker energy to manifest into my reality in the form of an unplanned pregnancy. Lesson ten is that when we fall in love with life, we don't need to know why something doesn't feel good, we can just get the heck out.

Unfortunately with Ella's dad, I didn't have the emotional maturity or the commitment to myself to avoid compromising my character for someone else's desires. I didn't have the wisdom to understand this was not a relationship for me to invest my time in the way I did. However, in this beautiful story, I was gifted the lesson to no longer have the desire to fall in love with someone, but to align myself to fall in love with every moment of my beautiful life. For that, I am eternally grateful.

It is from that moment of eternal gratitude that true beauty is born—when we allow ourselves to receive the small moments of falling in love with life. From this space, the natural laws of the universe will show up for you, giving you the opportunity to co-create with another human and an honest commitment to fall in love over and over again, regardless of what variables exist in a present reality. Remember, only you can choose to move from a compromised life to *An Uncompromised Life*. Only you can choose to be committed to falling in love with life, not people. It's when you choose this that you become your own hero, where you pull your dream world into your reality, to truly create the most phenomenal, uncompromised life.

CHAPTER 12

Start Creating Instead of Doing

Lesson eleven: One of the most powerful things about becoming pregnant and what it taught me is learning there are two ways to live life. There is a way to live from *creating*, and a way to live from *doing*.

If I would have kept my sweet Ella, I would have just been "doing" life because the things that happened were unexpected, and I would have allowed them to take over my life. I would have gone through the motions of being a mom within a lifestyle infrastructure where I was not ready to be a mom. I was not ready to forgo my big dreams and plans to serve the world in place of being in an unhappy relationship dynamic for at least twenty years, reminding me of the mistake I had allowed myself to live through with the father.

I would have just *done* life, instead of *creating* life . . .

A great example of *doing* life is when you wake up, snooze your alarm clock, rush to cook breakfast, rush to do everything for everyone else, rush to show up for work, rush to answer the phone, and before you know it, you just completed a whole day of *doing* rather than actually slowing down to see all the opportunities you had to create a different reality.

In order to become who you are truly meant to be in this world, you must stop doing and allow yourself to become the creator. Now, the lifestyle of becoming a creator may seem like it's so far away that you cannot grasp it or even think to yourself, "How can this become my reality?"

Everything starts in small moments. The average person lives 27,375 days before their time is up. Within these days, life is filled with moments—twenty-four hours in a day, sixty minutes in an hour, and sixty seconds in a minute. What we do with each second—from the thoughts we have to the words we speak and with whom we spend our time—is what forms our reality. We're either being task-driven—running through the motions, or being creative-driven—allowing a greater energy to move through us and create a life around us.

For example, when my phone rings and it's a friend I haven't heard from in a while or even a friend I haven't spoken with often, and I am in the middle of cooking, cleaning, showering, or any other self-care task but feel the *need* to answer to be there for that friend, I just stepped into *doing* mode.

This is stepping into doing instead of creating because you are showing up to fulfill a validation, born from wanting to be needed, avoiding loneliness, or escaping the reality of the false perception that you may be that person who can fix everything for everyone. This speaks to owning our true value, instead of getting lost in our false illusion of innocence.

You can stop the doing and stop your suffering by simply slowing down and asking yourself this one question: "Is the action I am about to *do* going to create a reality that I want to live in?" The answer is a simple yes or no.

Many times, for me, saying no is more challenging then saying yes. Why? Because we have all sorts of programs running in us, such as:

➤ People pleasing
➤ Needing to be validated
➤ Desiring to be wanted
➤ Avoiding responsibility for our reality
➤ Codependency

When we slow down to ask ourselves better questions, to allow more expansive thoughts to come through us, and to receive answers that feel better, we move into a creative state.

For example, this whole story could have happened *to* me. Instead, I made it *for* me and for others. I created it as part of my story, instead of doing the pregnancy because it was what someone else wanted, or doing the abortion and hiding from it to get through life. I chose to create this traumatic life experience to become a beautiful space where Ella became real. We each have opportunities in every moment to *create* our life, rather than going through the motions of *doing* it.

I created this book as my healing journey. I created the support systems I needed to get through this. I didn't keep doing a relationship that was not working for me. I didn't do a baby because it was what the world thinks I should have done. I created the reality where I shifted generational lineage, completed my soul contract and karmic debt, and naturally the laws of the universe showed up to support me. The world gave me divine confirmation that I was creating the right path for me by allowing the name Ella to be birthed through the little girl, Ella's dad, and my mom. Then there was the magical letter I was mailed from a woman I had never heard of, containing $245 in baby gift cards. This all showed me that I was creating my life my way instead of doing it someone else's way. I promise you, when you start to choose yourself and create for yourself, these same signs and unexplainable confirmations from the universe will show up for you.

Throughout my story, I became committed to creating my life by putting myself before everyone else. It doesn't mean that I still have unconscious or conscious moments where I turn a blind eye or a deaf ear—*doing* something instead of *creating,* because I choose not to listen to my internal system. It just means when I live my life doing, a huge lesson or sign appears for me to get back into alignment with being the creator of my life. And I'm able to recognize those signs and lessons much quicker than I was before this story occurred.

For example, when I left the corporate matrix in January 2018, I knew from that moment forward that no matter what happened to me in my life, going back to a "real" job would never happen for me. I knew that I was going to *create* success my way instead of *doing* "successful" things I was programmed and trained to do. Well, I have learned many lessons between 2018 and 2020—the year I am writing this book—because I still *did* things to find success instead of *creating* things to solve people's problems. When you are not solving other people's problems, I learned this is what causes you to go into $100,000 in debt. Money is simply a frequency that you can receive when you have created a solution to people's problems. The less money you have, the less you are creating solutions to solve people's problems, and the more you are simply just doing life.

This can be tricky to know what doing versus creating means for you. Everyone's way of doing and creating is different because of their own inner guidance system. The tricky, yet also divinely amazing part about living *An Uncompromised Life* is there is no right or wrong way for every single person to create it—because each person is unique. Every person has their own inner guidance system, so the same event can happen to two people and they can have vastly different results.

My own example is worth repeating. Another woman might decide to keep an unplanned baby and create an amazing life from it, be an amazing mom, build a great new relationship, work with co-parenting, and it all results in a beautiful life. That mom may start a business for moms, she may lead a workout class for moms . . . who really knows? The point is: She creates her life around being a mom, because that's what she truly saw for herself in the world.

One woman decides to let go of the baby and creates an amazing life with her vision of how she wants to live her life, how she wants to meet the right partner, how she has a business or life that she is madly in love with, and maybe she'll try again one day for a baby . . . or maybe not. Both women are living the definition of *An Uncompromised Life.*

There is no right or wrong, yet what was it that allowed both of these women to live a *An Uncompromised Life*? They both created a life they were proud to live and excited to remember.

It doesn't matter what you *do* in life, as long as you are creating a life from a place that feels good for you—not what feels good for everyone else. Because when you live from a place of doing just to get things done, moving through one task and on to the next, you cannot possibly be thriving in life. The whole point of having a human experience is to be present in your body—to receive all the things that this world can offer you. Yet, the world can only offer you opportunities that you are ready to receive.

Doing alone can create depression, worry, sadness, cancer, viruses that manifest in the body, and every other negative thing you can think of. The *doing* mentality creates the disembodiment and opportunity for dis-ease to manifest within the body, where *creating* allows you to co-create with the universe. Having ideas flow though you on how you can naturally create solutions to people's problems creates a life beyond your wildest dreams, because you start helping people in ways you never knew were possible.

If I would have become pregnant, chose to let Ella go, and go on with my life, I would have just allowed that to happen to me. Yet in talking with my mum, healing our relationship at a deeper level, creating this book, and creating the CrystELLA line . . . *this* is how I created my life around an unfortunate event. The difference is: I created it my way instead of allowing someone else to simply use me in the creation of their life, without intentionally asking me if I was even willing to live that life with them!

By choosing to create all of these beautiful ways to serve other people, empower them, help them understand their beautiful emotions, and help them recognize the things moving through their minds, my life became magical. We each can take our creative life force power back, and chose to live a life uncompromised to our soul's true desire.

That is what this is all about—there is no right or wrong way to do it, and there is no absolute truth. There is only the opportunity to choose to create a life you are proud to live, regardless of all the perceived bad moments. Go out there and make it magical. Go out there and win big. Go out there and live a life beyond your wildest dreams. Go out there and help people the best that you can. Wherever you are now is already a good enough place to start helping others and create a business from doing it.

Trust me, if I can pick myself up off the ground from crying and being heartbroken as many times as I have in my life and see many other people do it, I know your best is good enough to help someone at their lowest.

You are already whole.

You are complete.

You are more than enough.

You are worthy of living the most incredible life and knowing deep down only the best is yet to come—when you stop doing and start creating.

CHAPTER 13

Embrace the Infinite Support Existing Around You

The final chapter. It's the biggest and most important lesson I want to share with you. Lesson twelve is to surrender to the infinite support the universe is here to offer you and be forever grateful for it. A lot of times, people say we cannot get support because we do not have money for a mentor, a therapist, a personal trainer, a finance person, or we do not have good friends; yet the truth is you always have more than enough to receive the support you desire. When you commit to living *An Uncompromised Life,* the money always shows up for you to receive external support. Even when you don't believe you have the money or time to receive support, you can always find ways to allow yourself to receive the infinite, never-ending support that is available for you right now from the universe. For example, this book is part of the infinite support the universe is providing you on your journey. You think you don't have great friends, but then you're at a coffee shop and you authentically communicate what is on your heart and mind to a random stranger, and that same person provides you with support because they went through the pain you are going through. Before you know it, you just made a new friend. There is always more than enough support from the universe—all for free if you allow it in. And the universe will provide you with financial resources to receive the proper guidance. But, you have to commit to the universe; be truly committed to make it through your trauma, and as I've experienced, money shows up from the infinite support of the universe in miraculous ways.

I couldn't be here writing this book without my girlfriend who helped me while I was sobbing on the phone right before I took the pill. I wouldn't be here as the woman you see today—poised, healed, and whole—without my friend who came over the night the atomic bomb went off in my stomach. I wouldn't be here today without my two girlfriends who called me the day I blocked Ella's dad's number because they wanted to make sure I was okay because in their heart they felt I was in pain, having zero idea he just shared a vision he had of me dying. I wouldn't be here before you without a dear friend of mine who did energy work on me when all of this was happening. I wouldn't be here helping people if I didn't have my beautiful business Colleen Gallagher International and my clients, who inspire me to keep moving forward, guiding them to their breakthroughs. I wouldn't be here before you without the neurofeedback therapy, my therapist, my mentor, my incredible friends, a healer I've worked with, and my parents. I wouldn't be where I am today if there weren't for the many free online tools and videos from Melanie Tonia Evans, Dr. Joe Despenzia, Gabby Bernstein, Louise Hays, Abraham Hicks, and other specialized researchers focusing on trauma. However, it was in me becoming available to show up and being committed to my own healing that made the ultimate difference in the universe being able to support me—providing me with more than enough money to receive external support and guiding me to free resources online. I spent countless hours (nights) reading, writing, and watching videos because I was committed to coming out of this life experience stronger and living a life beyond what I ever imagined was possible.

I am here in front of you living *An Uncompromised Life* because I had so much support—people who pushed me through this with tough love, who listened to me when I was in so much pain from a broken heart, and who gave me hope when I couldn't find it in myself. I had so many miraculous people show up for me. I had the universe give me three confirmations of the name Ella, the pink card from a random woman (containing $245 in baby gift cards) to know this was part of a greater collective healing, this book come through me so quickly, a publishing house ready to get this out, the random man who happened to be in the elevator with me after I took the first pill—simply hugging me while I was sobbing and he had no idea what was happening, COVID-19 occurring for me to really heal and not suppress this, and the list goes on. There was so much infinite support that showed up for me, because for the first time in my life, the brilliant woman whose life always seemed so perfect had to admit that she needed help. It was in my vulnerability of admitting I needed help, support, and people to guide me back to wholeness, that this infinite amount of support showed up through people, money, and experiences. All I had to do was show up, be committed to going through the feelings, trust the process of healing, and believe this is what it takes to live *An Uncompromised Life*.

I know whatever it is you are going through, infinite support is available to you right now as well. Just go into your heart, ask yourself what you're feeling, what it is you need, and who is it you can reach out to. Then absolutely make it happen—change your life to live the life you always deserved to live in the first place. From this place of receiving support in your life, no longer allowing yourself to go through life alone, I promise you, you will never again compromise your character to fit someone else's desires because you will have so many people around you reminding you how important it is for you to show up as you, in the greater equation of the universe.

My greatest message to offer you though this lesson is to never let anything destabilize you. I've come to terms with where I am heading in this lifetime, that is what was required of me to go through this pain now—so I could master my emotions and know how important it is to always put myself first. If I went through this, and I can still be the incredible human I am today, I know I'm unstoppable against anything that is yet to come. That is the best miracle the universe could give me—or anyone. I never thought I could get pregnant, yet I did, and I still made my choice. Now, I know there is nothing in the world that can happen to me to destabilize me from completing my divine mission—my soul contract—and creating *An Uncompromised Life* . . . my way. I am worthy of all my dreams and you are too. I hope through this story you have found the same hope, strength, and determination to make your life uncompromised to your soul and to enjoy every sparkle-filled moment . . . because you deserve it.

In all of this, my intention and greatest desire is for you to see whatever pain and trauma you have gone through, you can absolutely start to rise up again. You can start right now—in this moment—to live *An Uncompromised Life*. You do not need to wait for more money, you do not need to suffer a day longer, you do not need to wait until your dreams come true, and you do not need to wait until you retire. Right now is the moment you start practicing being true to who you are.

I have released my greatest false illusion of a love saga that has gone on for centuries and centuries. In the past, I always chose to be the slave girl, the healer, the one who was hushed away to make sure everything looked nice and pretty—for everyone else to shine. I've been burnt at the stake more times than I can count, yet I've also been the murderer. I've been raped, and I've been the person who has raped in past lifetimes.

Yet through this journey, I have discovered what it means to live *An Uncompromised Life*—to be given the gift of knowing that I can become pregnant without needing medical pills. From this newfound awareness of what it means to create my version of *An Uncompromised Life,* it allowed me to let go of the false idea of what a love story should feel like and my karmic debt through this trauma is now complete—the debt I suffered from my mum's generational lineage of people pleasing, codependency, and putting others before one's Self; the debt that I needed to compromise myself in order to receive validation from a toxic love story.

My decision of creating a life with my sweet Ella in the realms unknown to most humans (yet everyone can tap into) was my greatest gift. Because in that process, I found me, and I freed my angel from having to suffer through any generational lineage and programming—seeing me suffer through living a life and relationship I would not have been happy with, and unhealed karmic debt. Ella's dad said it beautifully, "You can have your cake and eat it too." That is exactly what it takes to live *An Uncompromised Life.*

It is to know what is best for you and to stop at nothing until you reach an empowered, peaceful, and whole state. It's to have the courage to choose yourself when no one else will. It's to drag yourself out of bed when the world seems to be crumbling. It's to know that everything realigns, harmonizes, and comes together better than we can ever imagine.

I hope through my great story, you see the power in following your heart, the courage it takes to be an empowered human, the opportunity you have to always recreate your life in every moment, and that you are able to truly live a life uncompromised to your soul's truest desires. Be selfishly self-less and know, my darling, you deserve to have your cake, sprinkle it with magical stardust, and eat it, too.

To My Beloved,

This is the fully story that was only between God and me. I cannot deliver all the answers of why things happen for us in our life, but I can share with you the story God presented me.

From the moment I saw you I fell in love with those black squiggly eyes. It's something about how the universe delivers exactly who we need in this human experience. Something I cannot explain but I feel it so deeply. Unfortunately, this story was written in the stars to break a curse for both of us. I knew our love story that's gone on for centuries, but I never felt safe enough to communicate it.

The moment you asked me, "What would you do if you walked in on me having sex with another woman?"

I wasn't upset because of the question it's because I intuitively and psychically knew you were asking me to do something, I never wanted to experience with you. And when it happened, I knew it was pre-planned by the Universe for me to betray myself to please you.

But I didn't know how to communicate it.

I thought if I just kept showing up things would get better.

But in reality, I just kept traumatizing myself and everyone involved.

When you were meant to come over after the movies and you said, "we are on the way."

I thought it confirmed that you didn't care about me.

Because you already made it a standard to only hang out with me when you were with her.

My heart broke a million times in so many moments, but I kept the pain to myself because you trained me when you said, "I don't have these problems in my life."

So, I stopped sharing myself because I didn't want to be another problem in your life. I wanted to be a gift.

In so many ways, I compromised my character, desires, and needs so your relationship with her was never impacted by me. I pretended my heart didn't break when I saw the way you looked at her vs me. I pretended to get up and leave early because I was repulsed by my own actions.

Love is sacred to me.

I told you this many times.

Yet I knew you weren't hearing me.

The moment you said, "I invited a friend over to the pool," and she walked out the front of your house instead of downstairs, from your room, I lost all trust.

It was in that moment, in the pool, God told me, I was the woman you were trying to get pregnant to have your and her child. I knew to stay far away from you as that was a life I did not want. But I couldn't stay away when you kept asking me to come near. I could only stay away when you left me alone. My emotions became crazy because I didn't know how to get out of this mess. I resented you every time you tried to get me to enter into your field of work, because I knew you weren't listening to my story or my Earth calling. Again, I felt unseen.

You saw me as a muse to squeeze the most out of to get your way with me and my talents. I never showed you the Real me because I knew I wasn't safe. Yet I kept trying to convince myself I was, but you always had unspoken intentions with my mind and body for your benefit. Hence the card the woman sent from your state, whom your friends with on Facebook, with an avocado on it, knowing you love avocado toast.

You knew my body language communicated fight or flight all the time because of your love for people. But it didn't faze you because your intention was to squeeze everything, I could offer into your life for you. I thought this pain and punishment was a form of love through society.

I shared a piece of my beautiful heart with you the day I took you to the 7th Ray Inn and the crystals but then you bought a gift for someone else, took my crystal I bought for myself, and then invited her for all of us to go to my special place I shared with you. Again, taking everything, I had to offer and giving it away.

Then I became pregnant with your child exactly what I envisioned 3 months earlier from God. Confirming you planned this for my life without talking to me. You again confirmed this when you jokily asked, "How much could I have paid you to keep the baby?"

As if I was just a body at your disposal.

I called to tell you and you hung up on me because you were "sick."

I called you again a couple days later and it said USER UNAVAILABLE.

A day later you asked, "How was your day?"

I replied, "Today was intense."

Of course, you didn't care to ask why.

I sat outside the clinic holding my phone screaming for you to call me if I was meant to have this child.

I was begging God for you to call as you've called many times before when I energetically asked you too.

And NOTHING…

The phone didn't ring.

A little girl sat right in front of me and it was the first time I felt our daughters Soul.

They called my name.

I went into the room sobbing, but you trained me, "I don't have these problems in my life."

She said, "Colleen you don't have to take this pill."

A flash, came in front of my eyes, when I was freezing on Halloween.

Another woman came over to make me warm.

You looked at the other woman you were dating and said, "Are you cold do you want my jacket?"

She said, "No."

You asked her again as I sat there cold while this other woman held me.

Then your friend who had 5 girlfriends there gave me his jacket because he noticed I was freezing.

Then the flash of my birthday came when you forgot your wallet and I paid for our time together, while the other woman you were dating went out and got my gifts.

So, I came back in my body I swallowed the pill and said, "I cannot have his baby."

Again, for God to choose those words out of my mouth it was never about me.

It was about you.

You called me, the morning after pill two, when an atomic bomb went off in my stomach, but I still showed up to a networking event the next day. Because I'm committed to my purpose.

And you said, "I've been thinking if I want you in my life, and I do."

GREAT!

I am glad you decided I'm worthy to be in your life now after you hung up on me, and your phone says USER unavailable, I told you my day was intense, and you didn't care to ask why.

So, I listened to you – I gave you the space to talk about our relationship.

Then I shared the news.

You said, "I need space."

As I cried my eyes out for 5 days until you came back to LA.

But the moment you needed me to help you with your book you flew back the next day.

Because you simply cared about the value I would bring to your life.

But though it all thank you.

Thank you for showing me how abundant I am when I asked for ZERO financial support and gave you my gifts for free.

Thanks for showing me how resilient I am.

Thanks for giving me my daughters Soul I get to adopt in my life story.

Thank you for showing me I am so divinely incredible to stand back up after my heart was shattered.

Thanks for letting me lie alone in bed crying while you were out traveling.

Thanks for showing me everything love is not.

Thanks for showing me how the Devil lives inside those who are weak and uncommitted to the work of God.

Most importantly thanks for showing me what forgiveness really looks like when someone tries to destroy you.

Live an incredible life, and I hope no one ever attacks your heart the way you did mine, because I know you don't have the strength to get back up with Grace. And in my heart, I love you, but it would never be enough to fill your empty Soul.

Enjoy every moment of this beautiful life.

All the best with all my love,
Colleen

About the Author

Colleen is passionate about empowering people to create heart-centered businesses that impact the world.

She became passionate about this after surviving childhood cancer and was able to get off the medication she was told she would be on for the rest of her life. She was also told it would be challenging for her to have children; yet, pregnancy became possible and she chose to let her first child go.

Colleen values being a global citizen traveling to over forty countries by age twenty-six. She has a B.A. in Marketing, an M.S. in Global Technology and Development and is pursuing her Ph.D. in Psychology with a focus on global leadership and change. Yet Colleen's greatest success is seeing her clients' businesses impact the world in a way that feels good for them.

Colleen empowers leaders and businesses to come to a newfound clarity of their life mission—the reason they are here on the planet—so they can impact the world. Colleen does this by guiding people to understand the gifts the universe has given them so they can take calculated action to grow their businesses and make an impact on the social injustices of the world. Her work involves teaching leaders to overcome heart-breaking and traumatic life events, and to then use their voices to attract community and opportunities to make a difference in this world.